The Complete Heart Healthy Air Fryer Cookbook

1500 Days of Easy and Nutritious Meals with 28-day Meal Plan to Master Heart-Healthy Cooking with Your Air Fryer | Full Color Edition

Elizabeth E. Wright

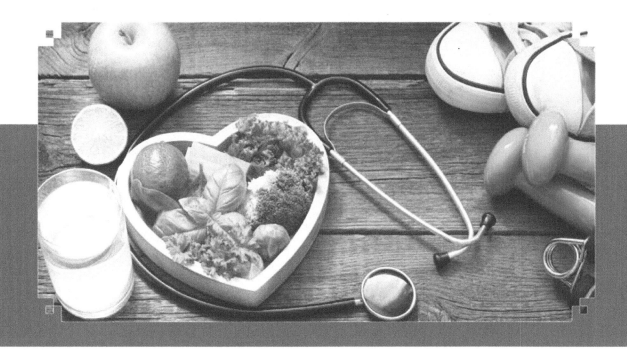

Manufactured in: USA

Cover Art: DANIELLE REES

Production Editor: SIENNA ADAMS

Production Manager: SARAH JOHNSON

Interior Design: DANIELLE REES

Art Producer: BROOKE WHITE

Editor: AALIYAH LYONS

Photography: MICHAEL SMITH

Table Of Contents

Introduction

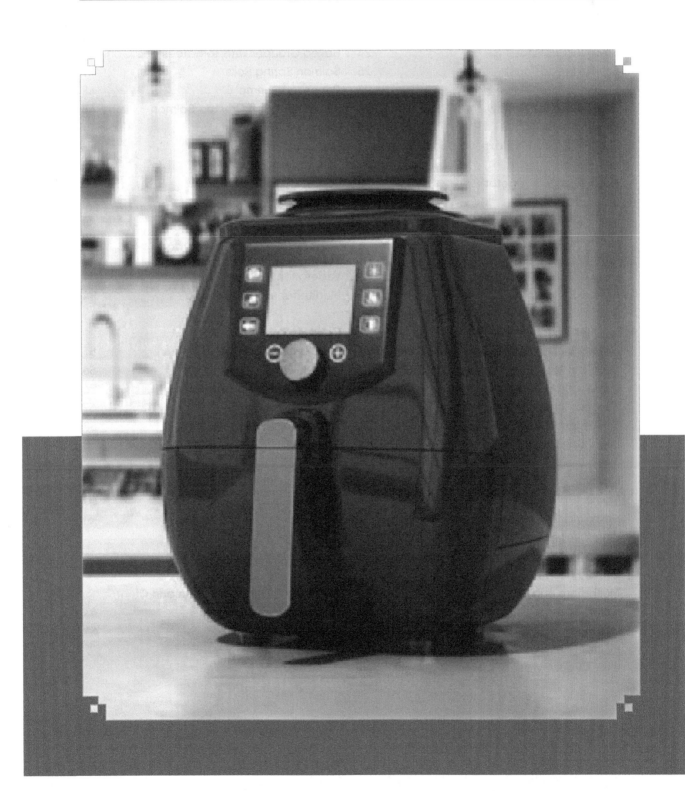

Stepping off that scale and hearing "obesity" and "heart disease" thrown around was a reality check that hit harder than a brick. Fear settled in my gut faster than a plate of greasy fries. But the doctor didn't shove me a diet plan and call it a day. Instead, he talked about "heart-healthy eating." Sounded boring, right? Well, let me tell you, it turned out to be way more interesting than I thought.

At first, I wasn't exactly sold. But the more I researched, the more it clicked. This wasn't about starving myself; it was about fueling my body with good stuff. We're talking colorful plates piled high with juicy fruits, rainbow veggies, and lean protein like fish and beans – way more exciting than the usual burger and fries routine. Sugary drinks? Out the door. In came water infused with fruits and herbs, surprisingly refreshing!

Let's be honest, the first few weeks were a bit of an adjustment. Portion control became my new best friend. I discovered whole grains like quinoa and brown rice, and healthy fats like avocados and nuts became my new pantry staples. Turns out, healthy food can be seriously delicious! Planning meals even became kind of fun, like a recipe treasure hunt. Who knew healthy could be so tasty?

Six months later, I was back at the doctor's office, feeling a mix of nervousness and hope. Then, he gave me the news – not only had the pounds started melting away, but my blood pressure and cholesterol were looking fantastic too! The fear that had been gripping me was replaced by a lightness I hadn't felt in years. It wasn't just about the weight loss; I felt like a whole new me.

and that's why I'm sharing this with you. Because this journey wasn't just for me. It showed me that healthy eating isn't a punishment, it's a way to feel amazing. Forget the fad diets and boring restrictions, let's explore the world of heart-healthy food that actually tastes good! This book is packed with easy recipes and tips I picked up along the way. So, join me on this adventure – let's transform our plates, one delicious bite at a time, and feel our best selves again.

Dedication

To David, I have to give a huge shoutout to my amazing husband. Remember how I mentioned those crispy, flavorful meals I can whip up in minutes? Well, a big part of that magic comes from the best birthday present ever – my air fryer! David surprised me with it, and let me tell you, it's been a game-changer. Now I can enjoy perfectly cooked veggies and lean proteins with minimal oil, making healthy meals even easier and tastier. It's become my go-to kitchen gadget, and it's helped me stay on track with healthy eating without sacrificing flavor. Thanks for always believing in me, David, and for finding the perfect tool to fuel this journey!

Chapter 1

Building a Heart-Healthy Plate with Your Air Fryer

Getting Started with Your Air Fryer

Congratulations on joining the air fryer revolution! This countertop appliance is changing the way we cook, offering delicious, crispy results with a fraction of the oil used in traditional frying. But before you dive headfirst into a basket full of tempting recipes, let's explore the essentials of using your air fryer effectively.

THE AIR FRYER ADVANTAGE

The air fryer has taken the culinary world by storm, promising a world of crispy, delicious food without the guilt of deep frying. But its appeal goes beyond just replicating the taste of deep-fried favorites. This countertop appliance offers a multi-faceted approach to healthier cooking, making it a valuable addition to any kitchen.

REDUCED FAT AND CALORIES

The heart of the air fryer's advantage lies in its cooking method. Unlike deep fryers, which completely submerge food in hot oil, air fryers rely on rapidly circulating hot air. This intense air circulation creates a Maillard reaction, browning the food's exterior while leaving the interior moist and flavorful. The key difference? Minimal oil is needed.

This translates to a significant reduction in fat and calories compared to traditional frying. Studies have shown that air frying can cut fat content by up to 70-80% and calorie intake by a similar margin. This makes air frying ideal for those seeking to manage their weight, lower cholesterol levels, or simply eat a more heart-healthy diet.

UNLOCKING FLAVORFUL VERSATILITY

The air fryer's capabilities extend far beyond mimicking deep-fried textures. Its ability to circulate hot air allows for a surprising variety of cooking methods. From perfectly golden french fries and crispy chicken wings to roasted vegetables, tender fish fillets, and even baked goods, the air fryer can handle a wide range of dishes.

This versatility makes it a true kitchen workhorse. You can whip up quick and healthy weeknight meals, prepare delicious appetizers for entertaining, or even experiment with baking healthier versions of your favorite desserts. The possibilities are endless, allowing you to explore new flavors and textures while staying true to your health goals.

FASTER COOKING TIMES

Time is a precious commodity in today's fast-paced world. One of the air fryer's advantages is its ability to cook food quickly and efficiently. Its compact size allows for rapid preheating compared to a conventional oven, and the concentrated airflow cooks food faster as well. This means you can enjoy delicious, home-cooked meals without spending hours in the kitchen.

Air fryers are perfect for busy weeknights when time is of the essence. They can also be a lifesaver when you have unexpected guests and need to whip up a quick and impressive appetizer. The speed of the air fryer allows you to prepare healthy, home-cooked meals without compromising on convenience.

PROMOTING HEALTHIER CHOICES

Air fryers aren't just about replicating indulgent treats in a healthier way. They can also be instrumental in encouraging healthier cooking choices overall. The ability to achieve crispy, satisfying textures with minimal oil makes air fryers a great alternative to unhealthy frying methods.

This can lead to a shift towards healthier ingredients and meal planning. with the air fryer, you can explore recipes that incorporate lean proteins, colorful vegetables, and whole grains, knowing they will still come out crispy and flavorful. This shift in cooking methods can have a positive impact on your overall dietary choices.

CONVENIENCE AND EASE OF USE

Additionally, air fryers are generally user-friendly appliances. Many models come with simple dials or digital controls, making them easy to operate for cooks of all experience levels. This convenience encourages healthier cooking habits by streamlining the cooking process and minimizing post-meal cleanup.

ESSENTIAL AIR FRYER TECHNIQUES

While the air fryer promises delicious and healthy meals with minimal effort, mastering a few key techniques can truly elevate your cooking experience and ensure consistent, perfectly cooked food every time. Here are some essential air fryer techniques to remember:

PREHEATING: GETTING YOUR AIR FRYER READY FOR ACTION

Similar to preheating your oven, preheating your air fryer is crucial for optimal results. Preheating allows the internal temperature to reach the desired level before you add your food, ensuring even cooking and crisping right from the start. Most air fryers take just 3-5 minutes to preheat, but always refer to your user manual for specific preheating instructions and recommended temperatures.

SHAKING AND FLIPPING: ENSURING EVEN COOKING AND CRISPNESS

For thicker foods like chicken breasts, vegetables, or even frozen fries, shaking or flipping your food halfway through the cooking process is essential. This ensures even exposure to the hot air circulating within the basket, leading to consistent browning and crisping on all sides.

How often you shake depends on the size and thickness of your food. Smaller items like fries might only need a shake once or twice, while thicker cuts of meat could benefit from shaking every 5-7 minutes. Use heat-resistant utensils like silicone tongs or a dedicated air fryer spatula to gently shake the basket and avoid overcrowding.

MASTERING COOKING TIMES AND TEMPERATURE ADJUSTMENTS

Air fryer recipes often provide specific cooking times and temperatures. However, these can vary slightly depending on several factors – the size and thickness of your food, the amount of food in the basket, and even your specific air fryer model.

Here's where a little practice comes in handy. Start with the recommended settings and keep a close eye on your food. Use a food thermometer to check the internal temperature a few minutes before the suggested cooking time is complete. This allows you to adjust the cooking time or temperature in small increments if needed to ensure proper doneness. Remember, it's always better to start with a slightly lower temperature and shorter cooking time and adjust as needed, rather than overcook your food.

UNDERSTANDING BASKET CAPACITY: AVOIDING OVERCROWDING

One of the keys to achieving crispy air-fried perfection is avoiding overcrowding the basket. When there's too much food in the basket, air circulation is hindered, leading to uneven cooking and a steamed rather than crispy texture.

Always follow the manufacturer's recommendations regarding the maximum capacity of your air fryer basket. In general, aim for a single layer of food with some space between each piece for optimal results. If you're cooking a large batch, consider cooking in smaller batches to ensure proper air circulation.

CLEANING AND MAINTAINING YOUR AIR FRYER

Your air fryer is a valuable kitchen companion, offering delicious and healthy meals with minimal oil. But to ensure its longevity and optimal performance, proper cleaning and maintenance are essential. Here's a breakdown of how to keep your air fryer in top shape:

POST-COOKING CLEANING: A QUICK AND EASY ROUTINE

- **Safety First:** Always allow the air fryer to cool completely before cleaning. This prevents burns and makes handling the components easier.
- **Basket Bonanza:** Most air fryer baskets and accessories are dishwasher-safe for convenient cleaning. Simply remove them from the unit and load them onto the top rack of your dishwasher. For stubborn grease buildup, pre-soak the basket and accessories in warm, soapy water before placing them in the dishwasher.
- **Exterior Elegance:** Wipe down the exterior of the air fryer with a damp cloth to remove any splatters or food particles. Avoid using harsh chemicals or abrasive sponges, as these can damage the finish.

DEEP CLEANING FOR A FRESH START:

For tougher grease buildup or a deeper clean, you can tackle the following:
- **Heating Element:** While the heating element itself shouldn't be submerged, you can carefully remove any food debris with a damp cloth or soft brush.
- **Interior Wipe Down:** For the interior of the air fryer unit, use a damp cloth with a mild dish soap solution to wipe down surfaces. Avoid using excessive water and ensure the unit is completely dry before plugging it back in.

GENERAL MAINTENANCE TIPS:

- **Consult Your Manual:** Always refer to your air fryer's user manual for specific cleaning instructions and recommendations for your model. Some models might have detachable components or specific cleaning requirements.
- **Non-Stick TLC:** Remember, the basket and accessories often have a non-stick coating. Avoid using abrasive scrubbing pads or metal utensils, as these can scratch the coating and compromise its effectiveness.
- **Regular Oil Removal:** While the air fryer uses minimal oil, some residual oil can accumulate over time. To prevent smoke or burning during future use, wipe down the interior with a paper towel after a few cooking sessions to remove any excess oil.

LONG-TERM CARE FOR LASTING PERFORMANCE:

- **Store it Right:** When not in use, unplug your air fryer and store it in a cool, dry place. Avoid leaving it on the counter near a heat source.
- **Regular Inspection:** Occasionally check the power cord and plug for any signs of damage. If you notice any fraying or wear, discontinue use and contact the manufacturer for a replacement.

Essential Ingredients for Heart Health

The air fryer offers a fantastic way to prepare delicious meals without sacrificing your heart health. But just like with any cooking method, the ingredients you choose play a crucial role in creating heart-friendly dishes. Let's explore some essential ingredients that should be staples in your air fryer repertoire.

LEAN PROTEIN POWERHOUSES

FISH AND SEAFOOD

Rich in omega-3 fatty acids, particularly EPA and DHA, fish and seafood are superstars for heart health. These essential fats have been shown to reduce inflammation, lower bad cholesterol (LDL), and raise good cholesterol (HDL), all beneficial factors for a healthy heart.

Salmon, tuna, mackerel, sardines, and shrimp are excellent choices for the air fryer. You can air fry them whole, as fillets, or even in delicious fish tacos. Opt for minimal oil or a light coating of a heart-healthy oil like olive oil, and don't forget the heart-healthy seasonings like lemon pepper or dill.

CHICKEN AND TURKEY BREASTS

Skinless, boneless chicken and turkey breasts are excellent sources of lean protein, which is essential for building and maintaining muscle mass. Additionally, these cuts are naturally lower in fat, making them ideal for heart-healthy cooking.

Air frying offers a fantastic way to achieve juicy, flavorful chicken and turkey breasts without the added fat of traditional frying methods. Experiment with marinades, spice rubs, or air-frying them with heart-healthy vegetables like broccoli or asparagus for a complete and balanced meal.

LEAN GROUND MEAT

While not as lean as chicken breast, ground turkey or lean ground beef (at least 90% lean) can be incorporated into heart-healthy air fryer recipes when used strategically. These options offer versatility and can be seasoned with heart-healthy spices and herbs to create delicious burgers, meatballs, or even air-fried shepherd's pie.

The key with ground meat is to drain any excess fat after browning it in the air fryer. This ensures you're minimizing the amount of saturated fat in your final dish. Lean ground meat can be a good source of iron and protein, so including it in moderation can be part of a heart-healthy diet.

HEART-HEALTHY FATS

Not all fats are created equal. While saturated and trans fats can contribute to heart disease, unsaturated fats, particularly monounsaturated fats and polyunsaturated fats, are crucial for heart health.

OLIVE OIL

A staple in the Mediterranean diet, olive oil is rich in monounsaturated fats, which have been shown to lower LDL cholesterol and promote heart health. Use a light drizzle of olive oil when air frying to add flavor and moisture without adding excess saturated fat.

AVOCADOS

These creamy fruits are packed with healthy monounsaturated fats, fiber, and potassium. Though high in calories, avocados can be enjoyed in moderation. Slice them on top of your air-fried fish tacos or mash them for a healthy guacamole dip.

NUTS AND SEEDS

Almonds, walnuts, flaxseeds, and chia seeds are all excellent sources of healthy fats, fiber, protein, and essential nutrients. They can be enjoyed whole as a snack or sprinkled over your air-fried vegetables or salads for an added crunch and nutritional boost.

FRUITS AND VEGETABLES

Fiber plays a vital role in heart health by promoting healthy cholesterol levels and aiding in digestion. Fruits and vegetables are naturally low in fat and calories, making them essential for a heart-healthy diet.

COLORFUL VEGETABLES

Air frying offers a fantastic way to unlock the natural sweetness of vegetables. Think colorful bell peppers, broccoli florets, asparagus spears, or even Brussels sprouts. These vegetables air fry beautifully, becoming tender and flavorful with a satisfying crispness.

FRUITS

While some fruits may be too delicate for air frying, others can be incorporated into your heart-healthy air fryer recipes. Consider air-frying sliced apples or pears with a sprinkle of cinnamon for a healthy dessert option. Berries are another excellent choice, and can be added to air-fried yogurt parfaits for a breakfast rich in antioxidants and fiber.

Adding Flavor without the Guilt
Heart-healthy doesn't have to be bland! Experiment with a variety of herbs and spices to add flavor to your air-fried dishes. Garlic, ginger, turmeric, cumin, chili powder, paprika, and all your favorite herbs are excellent choices. Not only do they add flavor, but some herbs and spices offer additional health benefits like anti-inflammatory properties.

MINIMIZE ADDED SUGARS

Sugary sauces and dressings can easily sabotage your heart-healthy efforts. Instead, use natural sweeteners like a squeeze of fresh lemon or a sprinkle of maple syrup. You can also create your own heart-healthy vinaigrettes using olive oil, vinegar, and fresh herbs for a flavorful dressing.

BUILDING A BALANCED HEART-HEALTHY MEAL:

By incorporating a variety of these essential ingredients into your air fryer repertoire, you can create delicious and balanced meals that are good for your heart.

- **Focus on Lean Protein:** Choose lean protein sources like fish, chicken, or turkey breast as the foundation of your dish.
- **Don't Forget the Veggies:** Pair your lean protein with a generous serving of air-fried vegetables. This ensures you're getting a good dose of fiber and essential nutrients.
- **Healthy Fats in Moderation:** Include a small amount of healthy fats like olive oil, avocado, or nuts and seeds for flavor and added nutritional benefits.
- **Flavorful Touches:** Experiment with herbs, spices, and natural sweeteners to add flavor without compromising your heart-healthy goals.

Air Fryer Cooking Chart

Beef					
Item	**Temp (°F)**	**Time (mins)**	**Item**	**Temp (°F)**	**Time (mins)**
Beef Eye Round Roast (4 lbs.)	400 °F	45 to 55	Meatballs (1-inch)	370 °F	7
Burger Patty (4 oz.)	370 °F	16 to 20	Meatballs (3-inch)	380 °F	10
Filet Mignon (8 oz.)	400 °F	18	Ribeye, bone-in (1-inch, 8 oz)	400 °F	10 to 15
Flank Steak (1.5 lbs.)	400 °F	12	Sirloin steaks (1-inch, 12 oz)	400 °F	9 to 14
Flank Steak (2 lbs.)	400 °F	20 to 28			

Chicken					
Item	**Temp (°F)**	**Time (mins)**	**Item**	**Temp (°F)**	**Time (mins)**
Breasts, bone in (1 1/4 lb.)	370 °F	25	Legs, bone-in lb.)	380 °F	30
Breasts, boneless (4 oz)	380 °F	12	Thighs, boneless (1 1/2 lb.)	380 °F	18 to 20
Drumsticks (2 1/2 lb.)	370 °F	20	Wings (2 lb.)	400 °F	12
Game Hen (halved 2 lb.)	390 °F	20	Whole Chicken	360 °F	75
Thighs, bone-in (2 lb.)	380 °F	22	Tenders	360 °F	8 to 10

Pork & Lamb					
Item	**Temp (°F)**	**Time (mins)**	**Item**	**Temp (°F)**	**Time (mins)**
Bacon (regular)	400 °F	5 to 7	Pork Tenderloin	370 °F	15
Bacon (thick cut)	400 °F	6 to 10	Sausages	380 °F	15
Pork Loin (2 lb.)	360 °F	55	Lamb Loin Chops (1-inch thick)	400 °F	8 to 12
Pork Chops, bone in (1-inch, 6.5 oz)	400 °F	12	Rack of Lamb (1.5 - lb.)	380 °F	22
Flank Steak (2 lbs.)	400 °F	20 to 28			

Fish & Seafood					
Item	**Temp (°F)**	**Time (mins)**	**Item**	**Temp (°F)**	**Time (mins)**
Calamari (8 oz)	400 °F	4	Tuna Steak	400 °F	7 to 10
Fish Fillet (1-inch, 8 oz)	400 °F	10	Scallops	400 °F	5 to 7
Salmon, fillet (6 oz)	380 °F	12	Shrimp	400 °F	5
Swordfish steak	400 °F	10	Sirloin steaks (1-inch, 12 oz)	400 °F	9 to 14
Flank Steak (2 lbs.)	400 °F	20 to 28			

Vegetables					
INGREDIENT	**AMOUNT**	**PREPARATION**	**OIL**	**TEMP**	**COOK TIME**
Asparagus	2 bunches	Cut in half, trim stems	2 Tbsp	420°F	12-15 mins
Beets	1 1/2 lbs	Peel, cut in 1/2-inch cubes	1Tbsp	390°F	28-30 mins
Bell peppers (for roasting)	4 peppers	Cut in quarters, remove seeds	1Tbsp	400°F	15-20 mins
Broccoli	1 large head	Cut in 1-2-inch florets	1Tbsp	400°F	15-20 mins
Brussels sprouts	1lb	Cut in half, remove stems	1Tbsp	425°F	15-20 mins
Carrots	1lb	Peel, cut in 1/4-inch rounds	1 Tbsp	425°F	10-15 mins
Cauliflower	1 head	Cut in 1-2-inch florets	2 Tbsp	400°F	20-22 mins
Corn on the cob	7 ears	Whole ears, remove husks	1 Tbps	400°F	14-17 mins
Green beans	1 bag (12 oz)	Trim	1 Tbps	420°F	18-20 mins
Kale (for chips)	4 OZ	Tear into pieces, remove stems	None	325°F	5-8 mins
Mushrooms	16 OZ	Rinse, slice thinly	1 Tbps	390°F	25-30 mins
Potatoes, russet	1 1/2 lbs	Cut in 1-inch wedges	1 Tbps	390°F	25-30 mins
Potatoes, russet	1lb	Hand-cut fries, soak 30 mins in cold water, then pat dry	1/2 -3 Tbps	400°F	25-28 mins
Potatoes, sweet	1lb	Hand-cut fries, soak 30 mins in cold water, then pat dry	1 Tbps	400°F	25-28 mins
Zucchini	1lb	Cut in eighths lengthwise, then cut in half	1 Tbps	400°F	15-20 mins

Chapter 2

4-Week Meal Plan

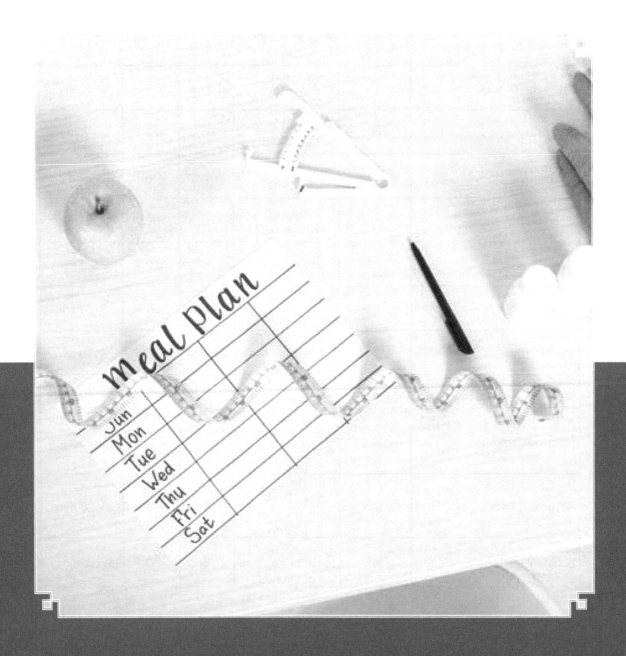

Week 1

DAY 1:
- Breakfast: Baked Peach Oatmeal
- Lunch: Beef Brisket Stew
- Snack: Zucchini Parmesan Chips
- Dinner: Salmon Nachos

Total for the day:
Calories: 853.30; Fat: 27.00;;Protein: 87.20; Carbs: 66.90; Fiber: 13.00

DAY 2:
- Breakfast: Baked Peach Oatmeal
- Lunch: Beef Brisket Stew
- Snack: Zucchini Parmesan Chips
- Dinner: Salmon Nachos

Total for the day:
Calories: 853.30; Fat: 27.00;;Protein: 87.20; Carbs: 66.90; Fiber: 13.00

DAY 3:
- Breakfast: Baked Peach Oatmeal
- Lunch: Beef Brisket Stew
- Snack: Zucchini Parmesan Chips
- Dinner: Salmon Nachos

Total for the day:
Calories: 853.30; Fat: 27.00;;Protein: 87.20; Carbs: 66.90; Fiber: 13.00

DAY 4:
- Breakfast: Baked Peach Oatmeal
- Lunch: Beef Brisket Stew
- Snack: Zucchini Parmesan Chips
- Dinner: Salmon Nachos

Total for the day:
Calories: 853.30; Fat: 27.00;;Protein: 87.20; Carbs: 66.90; Fiber: 13.00

DAY 5:
- Breakfast: Baked Peach Oatmeal
- Lunch: Beef Brisket Stew
- Snack: Zucchini Parmesan Chips
- Dinner: Vegetarian Chilli with Tofu

Total for the day:

Calories: 990.30; Fat: 35.00; Protein: 95.80; Carbs: 78.30; Fiber: 9.00

DAY 6:
- Breakfast: Baked Peach Oatmeal
- Lunch: Beef Brisket Stew
- Snack: Nutritious Roasted Chickpeas
- Dinner: Vegetarian Chilli with Tofu

Total for the day:
Calories: 1258.00; Fat: 43.70; Protein: 95.10; Carbs: 120.30; Fiber: 9.00

DAY 7:
- Breakfast: Spinach Frittata
- Lunch: Vegetarian Chilli with Tofu
- Snack: Nutritious Roasted Chickpeas
- Dinner: Vegetarian Chilli with Tofu

Total for the day:
Calories: 1281.00; Fat: 59.80; Carbs: 119.10; Protein: 51.50; Fiber: 5.00

Week 2

DAY 1:
- Breakfast: Vegetable Shrimp Toast
- Lunch: Herbed Roasted Chicken
- Snack: Kale Chips with Tex-Mex Dip
- Dinner: Italian-Style Burgers

Total for the day:
Calories: 1599.00; Fat: 86.90; Carbs: 48.60; Protein: 112.70; Fiber: 7.70

DAY 2:
- Breakfast: Vegetable Shrimp Toast
- Lunch: Herbed Roasted Chicken
- Snack: Kale Chips with Tex-Mex Dip
- Dinner: Italian-Style Burgers

Total for the day:
Calories: 1599.00; Fat: 86.90; Carbs: 48.60; Protein: 112.70; Fiber: 7.70

DAY 3:
- Breakfast: Vegetable Shrimp Toast
- Lunch: Herbed Roasted Chicken

- Snack: Kale Chips with Tex-Mex Dip
- Dinner: Italian-Style Burgers

Total for the day:

Calories: 1599.00; Fat: 86.90; Carbs: 48.60; Protein: 112.70; Fiber: 7.70

DAY 4:
- Breakfast: Vegetable Shrimp Toast
- Lunch: Herbed Roasted Chicken
- Snack: Kale Chips with Tex-Mex Dip
- Dinner: Italian-Style Burgers

Total for the day:

Calories: 1599.00; Fat: 86.90; Carbs: 48.60; Protein: 112.70; Fiber: 7.70

DAY 5:
- Breakfast: Mixed Veggie Hash
- Lunch: Herbed Roasted Chicken
- Snack: Kale Chips with Tex-Mex Dip
- Dinner: Greek Chicken Kebabs

Total for the day:

Calories: 1340.50; Fat: 57.80; Carbs: 44.90; Fiber: 9.00; Protein: 123.50

DAY 6:
- Breakfast: Mixed Veggie Hash
- Lunch: Herbed Roasted Chicken
- Snack: Kale Chips with Tex-Mex Dip
- Dinner: Greek Chicken Kebabs

Total for the day:

Calories: 1340.50; Fat: 57.80; Carbs: 44.90; Fiber: 9.00; Protein: 123.50

DAY 7:
- Breakfast: Mixed Veggie Hash
- Lunch: Herbed Roasted Chicken
- Snack: Kale Chips with Tex-Mex Dip
- Dinner: Greek Chicken Kebabs

Total for the day:

Calories: 1340.50; Fat: 57.80; Carbs: 44.90; Fiber: 9.00; Protein: 123.50

Week 3

DAY 1:
- Breakfast: Cranberry Bread
- Lunch: Turkey Meatballs
- Snack: Cheesy Hot Sauce Collard Chips
- Dinner: Crispy Garlic Sliced Eggplant

Total for the day:

Calories: 906.70; Fat: 38.60; Carbs: 107.60; Protein: 49.10; Fiber: 15.40

DAY 2:
- Breakfast: Cranberry Bread
- Lunch: Turkey Meatballs
- Snack: Cheesy Hot Sauce Collard Chips
- Dinner: Crispy Garlic Sliced Eggplant

Total for the day:

Calories: 906.70; Fat: 38.60; Carbs: 107.60; Protein: 49.10; Fiber: 15.40

DAY 3:
- Breakfast: Cranberry Bread
- Lunch: Turkey Meatballs
- Snack: Cheesy Hot Sauce Collard Chips
- Dinner: Crispy Garlic Sliced Eggplant

Total for the day:

Calories: 906.70; Fat: 38.60; Carbs: 107.60; Protein: 49.10; Fiber: 15.40

DAY 4:
- Breakfast: Cranberry Bread
- Lunch: Turkey Meatballs
- Snack: Cheesy Hot Sauce Collard Chips
- Dinner: Crispy Garlic Sliced Eggplant

Total for the day:

Calories: 906.70; Fat: 38.60; Carbs: 107.60; Protein: 49.10; Fiber: 15.40

DAY 5:
- Breakfast: Cranberry Bread
- Lunch: Turkey Meatballs
- Snack: Cheesy Hot Sauce Collard Chips
- Dinner: Parmesan Shrimp

Total for the day:

Calories: 968.70; Fat: 45.90; Carbs: 94.10; Protein: 55.80; Fiber: 13.40

DAY 6:

- Breakfast: Cranberry Bread
- Lunch: Turkey Meatballs
- Snack: Dill Beet Chips
- Dinner: Parmesan Shrimp

Total for the day:

Calories: 962.80; Fat: 41.81; Carbs: 86.60; Protein: 49.90; Fiber: 7.60

DAY 7:

- Breakfast: Cranberry Bread
- Lunch: Parmesan Shrimp
- Snack: Dill Beet Chips
- Dinner: Parmesan Shrimp

Total for the day:

Calories: 948.80; Fat: 42.41; Carbs: 84.20; Protein: 37.70; Fiber: 9.30

Week 4

DAY 1:

- Breakfast: Southwest Egg Rolls
- Lunch: Greek Pork Gyros
- Snack: Cozy Apple Crisp
- Dinner: Nutty Chicken Nuggets

Total for the day:

Calories: 1276.00; Protein: 84.40; Fat: 41.90; Carbs: 145.70; Fiber: 13.90

DAY 2:

- Breakfast: Southwest Egg Rolls
- Lunch: Greek Pork Gyros
- Snack: Cozy Apple Crisp
- Dinner: Nutty Chicken Nuggets

Total for the day:

Calories: 1276.00; Protein: 84.40; Fat: 41.90; Carbs: 145.70; Fiber: 13.90

DAY 3:

- Breakfast: Southwest Egg Rolls
- Lunch: Greek Pork Gyros
- Snack: Cozy Apple Crisp
- Dinner: Nutty Chicken Nuggets

Total for the day:

Calories: 1276.00; Protein: 84.40; Fat: 41.90; Carbs: 145.70; Fiber: 13.90

DAY 4:

- Breakfast: Southwest Egg Rolls
- Lunch: Greek Pork Gyros
- Snack: Cozy Apple Crisp
- Dinner: Nutty Chicken Nuggets

Total for the day:

Calories: 1276.00; Protein: 84.40; Fat: 41.90; Carbs: 145.70; Fiber: 13.90

DAY 5:

- Breakfast: Southwest Egg Rolls
- Lunch: Cheesy Italian Squid
- Snack: Garlic Cauliflower Florets
- Dinner: Greek Fish Pita

Total for the day:

Calories: 1295.90; Protein: 79.60; Fat: 55.72; Carbs: 129.31; Fiber: 15.70

DAY 6:

- Breakfast: Southwest Egg Rolls
- Lunch: Cheesy Italian Squid
- Snack: Garlic Cauliflower Florets
- Dinner: Greek Fish Pita

Total for the day:

Calories: 1295.90; Protein: 79.60; Fat: 55.72; Carbs: 129.31; Fiber: 15.70

DAY 7:

- Breakfast: Southwest Egg Rolls
- Lunch: Cheesy Italian Squid
- Snack: Garlic Cauliflower Florets
- Dinner: Greek Fish Pita

Total for the day:

Calories: 1295.90; Protein: 79.60; Fat: 55.72; Carbs: 129.31; Fiber: 15.70

Chapter 3

Appetizers and Desserts

Cinnamon Toast Granola

Prep time: 15 minutes | Cook time: 10 minutes | Serves 4

- 2 tbsp. ground flaxseed
- 6 tbsp. warm water
- 3 cups gluten-free old-fashioned rolled oats
- ½ cup chopped pecans
- 1 cup unsweetened dried figs, chopped
- 2 tbsp. ground cinnamon
- 1 tbsp. dried ginger
- 1 tsp. pure vanilla extract
- ¼ tsp. sea salt
- 2½ tbsp. erythritol-stevia blend, such as truvia
- ¼ cup unsweetened applesauce

1. Preheat the air fryer to 350°F.
2. In a small bowl, stir together the ground flaxseed with the warm water and allow to sit for 10 minutes to thicken.
3. In a large bowl, stir together the oats, pecans, flax egg, figs, cinnamon, ginger, vanilla, and salt.
4. In a separate small bowl, stir together the erythritol-stevia blend and applesauce until the sweetener is dissolved, then add it to the oat mixture.
5. Line the air fryer basket with parchment paper. Working in batches if necessary, pour the granola mixture into the basket and level into an even layer. Cook for 7 minutes, until golden brown.
6. Remove the granola from the air fryer carefully and lay on the counter to cool.

PER SERVING

Calories: 432 | Fat: 16g | Carbs: 75g | Fiber: 13g | Protein: 11g

Apple Hand Pies

Prep time: 15 minutes | Cook time: 10 minutes | Serves 6

- 14 oz. refrigerated package pie crust (2 crusts)
- ½ (21 oz.) can of apple pie filling
- 2 tbsp. almond butter
- 3 tsp. turbinado sugar
- caramel sauce for dipping

1. At 350°F, preheat your air fryer.
2. Spread the pie crusts on the working surface.
3. Cut 5-inch circles out of the crusts using a cookie cutter.
4. Add two slices of apples from the pie filling at the center of each round.
5. Fold the dough circles in half and press edges with a fork to seal the filling.
6. Place the apple hand pies in the air fryer basket.
7. Brush the almond butter over the handpieces and drizzle sugar on top.
8. Cut 3 slits on top of each hand pie and air fry for 10 minutes.
9. Serve with caramel sauce.

PER SERVING

Calories: 349 | Fat: 13.5g | Carbs: 56.3g | Protein: 4.6g |Fiber: 1g

Garlic-Roasted Tomatoes and Olives

Prep time: 5 minutes | Cook time: 20 minutes | Serves 6

- 2 cups cherry tomatoes
- 4 garlic cloves, roughly chopped
- ½ red onion, roughly chopped
- 1 cup black olives
- 1 cup green olives
- 1 tbsp. fresh basil, minced
- 1 tbsp. fresh oregano, minced
- 2 tbsp. olive oil
- ¼ to ½ tsp. salt

1. Preheat the air fryer to 380°F.
2. In a large bowl, combine all of the ingredients and toss together so that the tomatoes and olives are coated well with the olive oil and herbs.
3. Pour the mixture into the air fryer basket, and roast for 10 minutes. Stir the mixture well, then continue roasting for an additional 10 minutes.
4. Remove from the air fryer, transfer to a serving bowl, and enjoy.

PER SERVING

Calories: 109 | Fat: 10g | Protein: 1g | Carbs: 6g | Fiber: 2g | Sugar: 2g

Veggie Frittata

Prep time: 10 minutes | Cook time: 8 to 12 minutes | Serves 4

- ½ cup chopped red bell pepper
- ⅓ cup minced onion
- ⅓ cup grated carrot
- 1 tsp. olive oil
- 6 egg whites
- 1 egg
- ⅓ cup 2 percent milk
- 1 tbsp. grated Parmesan cheese

1. In a 6-by-2-inch pan, stir together the red bell pepper, onion, carrot, and olive oil. Put the pan into the air fryer. Cook for 4 to 6 minutes, shaking the basket once, until the vegetables are tender.
2. Meanwhile, in a medium bowl, beat the egg whites, egg, and milk until combined.
3. Pour the egg mixture over the vegetables in the pan. Sprinkle with the Parmesan cheese. Return the pan to the air fryer.
4. Bake for 4 to 6 minutes more, or until the frittata is puffy and set.
5. Cut into 4 wedges and serve.

PER SERVING

Calories: 77| Fat: 3g | Protein: 8g| Carbs: 5g| Fiber: 1g

Mixed Veggie Hash

Prep time: 10 minutes | Cook time:30 minutes |Serves 4

- 2 cups cubed potatoes (or turnips or rutabagas or a combo)
- 2 cups cubed sweet potatoes (or carrots or beets or a combo)
- 2 tsp olive oil
- 1 tsp DIY Cajun Seasoning Blend (or use store-bought)
- 1 (15 to 20 oz) block super-firm or high-protein tofu cut into cubes or firm tofu pressed overnight (*or use 1½ cups cooked chickpeas)
- 2 tsp Breakfast Seasoning Mix

1. Toss the potatoes and sweet potatoes in a large bowl with the olive oil, if using, and the Cajun seasoning. Fill up your air fryer basket about halfway. Cook on 330°F for 10 minutes, shake, then cook 10 minutes more.
2. While the veggies are cooking, toss the tofu with the Breakfast Seasoning Mix. Add on top of the veggies and cook on 390°F for 5 minutes, then shake and cook for 5 minutes more.
3. Serve with a side of ketchup and some sautéed greens.

PER SERVING

Calories:281.5 | Fat:7.8g |Carbs: 37.5g | Fiber: 5.0g | Protein: 20.4g

Pumpkin Donut Holes

Prep time: 15 minutes | Cook time: 14 minutes | Makes 12 donut holes

- 1 cup whole-wheat pastry flour, plus more as needed
- 3 tbsp. packed brown sugar
- ½ tsp. ground cinnamon
- 1 tsp. low-sodium baking powder
- ⅓ cup canned no-salt-added pumpkin purée (not pumpkin pie filling; see Tip)
- 3 tbsp. 2 percent milk, plus more as needed
- 2 tbsp. unsalted butter, melted
- 1 egg white
- Powdered sugar (optional)

1. In a medium bowl, mix the pastry flour, brown sugar, cinnamon, and baking powder.
2. In a small bowl, beat the pumpkin, milk, butter, and egg white until combined. Add the pumpkin mixture to the dry ingredients and mix until combined. You may need to add more flour or milk to form a soft dough.
3. Divide the dough into 12 pieces. with floured hands, form each piece into a ball.
4. Cut a piece of parchment paper or aluminum foil to fit inside the air fryer basket but about 1 inch smaller in diameter. Poke holes in the paper or foil and place it in the basket.
5. Put 6 donut holes into the basket, leaving some space around each. Air-fry for 5 to 7 minutes, or until the donut holes reach an internal temperature of 200°F and are firm and light golden brown.
6. Let cool for 5 minutes. Remove from the basket and roll in powdered sugar, if desired. Repeat with the remaining donut holes and serve.

PER SERVING (2 DONUT HOLES)

Calories: 142 | Fat: 4g | Protein: 3g | Carbs: 23g | Fiber: 3g

Crispy Carrot Fries

Prep time: 10 minutes | **Cook time:** 20 minutes | Serves 4

- 3 large carrots, peel & cut into fries shape
- ½ tsp paprika
- ½ tsp onion powder
- 2 tbsp olive oil
- ¼ tsp chili powder
- 1 tsp garlic powder
- Pepper
- Salt

1. Preheat your air fryer to 350 F/ 180 C.
2. Tossing carrot fries with remaining ingredients in a mixing bowl until well coated.
3. Add carrot fries into the air fryer basket and cook for 15-20 minutes. Stir halfway through.
4. Serve and enjoy.

PER SERVING

Calories: 87 | Fat: 7.1 g | Carbs: 6.3 g | Sugar: 3 g | Protein: 0.7 g | Fiber: 0.8g

Lime Corn on the Cob

Prep time: 10 minutes | **Cook time:** 20 minutes |Serves 4

- 4 ears corn, husked and cleaned
- 1 lime, quartered
- Salt, to taste
- Optional spices like chili powder, cumin, garam masala or your favorite spice blend

1. Rub each ear of corn with a quarter of a lime, then sprinkle salt or your choice of seasoning over corn.
2. If the ears are too large to fit in your air fryer, you can cut them in hal°F. Add 2 to 4 ears into your air fryer basket. It will vary depending on the size you have.
3. Cook at 400°F (205°C) for 10 minutes. Turn using tongs and cook 5 to 10 minutes more until the corn is tender.

PER SERVING

Calories:85.0 | Fat:1.0g |Carbs: 19.8g | Fiber: 3.5g | Protein: 3.1g

Broccoli and Cheese Quiche

Prep time: 20 minutes | Cook time: 20 minutes |
Serves 2

- 2 eggs, beaten
- 1 cup of nonfat or low-fat milk
- 2 cups of steamed broccoli florets in the cup
- 1 cup Grated cheddar cheese
- 1 tomato, diced
- 1 tsp. of thyme that has been dried
- 1 tsp. of minced parsley
- If desired, season with salt and pepper to taste

1. Combine all of the components in a bowl and mix.
2. Place the mixture in a compact baking dish.
3. Put the pan in the air fryer and start cooking.
4. Prepare in an air fryer at a temperature of 360 °F for twenty minutes.
5. Crumbled feta cheese is a great topping option for this dish.
6. Preparation and cooking tips: You can substitute dairy milk with a nondairy alternative.

PER SERVING

Calories: 125 | Fat: 8g | Carbs: 1g | Protein: 12g | Sugar: 0g | Fiber: 0g

Vegetable Shrimp Toast

Prep time: 15 minutes | Cook time: 3 to 6 minutes
| Serves 4

- 8 large raw shrimp, peeled and finely chopped
- 1 egg white
- 2 garlic cloves, minced
- 3 tbsp. minced red bell pepper
- 1 medium celery stalk, minced
- 2 tbsp. cornstarch
- ¼ tsp. Chinese five-spice powder
- 3 slices firm thin-sliced no-sodium whole-wheat bread

1. In a small bowl, stir together the shrimp, egg white, garlic, red bell pepper, celery, cornstarch, and five-spice powder. Top each slice of bread with one-third of the shrimp mixture, spreading it evenly to the edges. with a sharp knife, cut each slice of bread into 4 strips.
2. Place the shrimp toasts in the air fryer basket in a single layer. You may need to cook them in batches. Air-fry for 3 to 6 minutes, until crisp and golden brown. Serve.

PER SERVING

Calories: 110|Fat: 2g | Protein: 9g|Carbs: 15g| Fiber: 2g

Blackberry Peach Cobbler

Prep time: 10 minutes | Cook time:20 minutes |Serves 4

- 1½ cups chopped peaches (cut into ½-inch thick pieces)
- 1 (6-ounce) package blackberries
- 2 tbsp. coconut sugar
- 2 tsp. arrowroot (or cornstarch)
- 1 tsp. lemon juice
- 2 tbsp. neutral-flavored oil (sunflower, safflower, or refined coconut)
- 1 tbsp. maple syrup
- 1 tsp. vanilla
- ½ cup rolled oats
- ⅓ cup whole-wheat pastry flour
- 3 tbsp. coconut sugar
- 1 tsp. cinnamon
- ¼ tsp. nutmeg
- ⅛ tsp. sea salt

1. In a 6-inch round, 2-inch deep baking pan, place the peaches, blackberries, coconut sugar, arrowroot, and lemon juice. Stir well with a rubber spatula, until thoroughly combined. Set aside.
2. In a separate bowl, combine the oil, maple syrup, and vanilla. Stir well. Add the oats, flour, coconut sugar, cinnamon, nutmeg, and salt. Stir well, until thoroughly combined. Crumble evenly over the peach-blackberry filling.
3. Bake for 20 minutes, or until the topping is crisp and lightly browned. Enjoy warm if at all possible, because it's beyond wonderful that way!

PER SERVING

Calories: 248 | Fat: 8g | Carbs: 42g | Fiber: 6g | Protein: 3g

Chapter 4

Breakfast

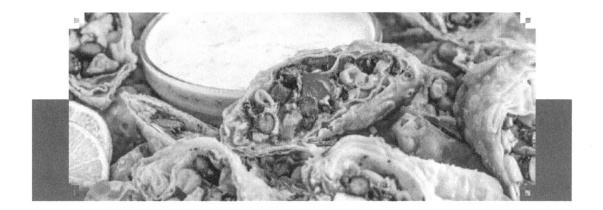

Southwest Egg Rolls

Prep time: 20 minutes | Cook time:15 minutes |Serves 10

- 1 cup frozen corn kernels, thawed
- 1 (15-ounce) can pinto beans, drained and rinsed
- ½ cup chopped plum tomatoes, drained
- 2 scallions, chopped
- 1 jalapeño pepper, minced
- 1½ cups shredded pepper Jack cheese
- 2 tsp. chili powder
- ½ tsp. dried oregano
- ¼ tsp. garlic powder
- 1 (20-count) package egg roll wrappers
- Cooking oil spray

1. In a large bowl, combine the corn, pinto beans, tomatoes, scallions, and jalapeño pepper until well mixed.
2. Add the cheese, chili powder, oregano, and garlic powder and mix well.
3. Place an egg roll wrapper on a work surface. Brush the edges with a bit of water, then place a heaping 2 tbsp. of the corn mixture in the middle. Fold one edge of the egg roll wrapper over the filling, fold in the sides, and roll up. Press the seam to secure. Repeat with the remaining filling and egg roll wrappers.
4. Set or preheat the air fryer to 375°F. Working in batches, put the egg rolls in the basket in a single layer, making sure they don't touch each other. Spray with cooking oil.
5. Place the basket in the air fryer and fry for 10 minutes. Remove the basket and turn the egg rolls over; spray them once more with oil. Return the basket and fry for another 5 minutes or until crisp. Repeat with remaining egg rolls. Let cool for 10 minutes, then serve.

PER SERVING
Calories: 376 | Protein: 17g | Fat: 6g |Carbs: 68g |Fiber: 5g

Baked Peach Oatmeal

Prep time: 5 minutes | Cook time: 30 minutes | Serves 6

- Olive oil cooking spray
- 2 cups certified gluten-free rolled oats
- 2 cups unsweetened almond milk
- ¼ cup raw honey, plus more for drizzling (optional)
- ½ cup nonfat plain Greek yogurt
- 1 tsp. vanilla extract
- ½ tsp. ground cinnamon
- ¼ tsp. salt
- 1½ cups diced peaches, divided, plus more for serving (optional)

1. Preheat the air fryer to 380°F. Lightly coat the inside of a 6-inch cake pan with olive oil cooking spray.
2. In a large bowl, mix together the oats, almond milk, honey, yogurt, vanilla, cinnamon, and salt until well combined.
3. Fold in ¾ cup of the peaches and then pour the mixture into the prepared cake pan.
4. Sprinkle the remaining peaches across the top of the oatmeal mixture. Bake in the air fryer for 30 minutes.
5. Allow to set and cool for 5 minutes before serving with additional fresh fruit and honey for drizzling, if desired.

PER SERVING

Calories: 197 | Fat: 3g| Protein: 9g | Carbs: 36g | Fiber: 4g

Breakfast Potatoes

Prep time: 10 minutes | Cook time: 20 minutes | Serves 6

- 1½ tsp. olive oil, divided
- 4 large potatoes, skins on, cut into cubes
- 2 tsp. seasoned salt, divided
- 1 tsp. minced garlic, divided
- ½ onion, diced
- 2 large green peppers, cut into 1-inch chunks

1. Drizzle the Air Fryer basket with olive oil.
2. In a bowl, mix the potatoes with ½ tsp. of oil. Sprinkle with 1 tsp. of seasoned salt and ½ tsp. of minced garlic. Mix to coat. Place the seasoned potatoes in the air fryer basket in a single layer. Cook for five minutes. Shake the basket and cook for another five minutes.
3. Meanwhile, stir the green peppers and onion with the remaining ½ tsp. of oil in a bowl.
4. Sprinkle the peppers and onions with the remaining 1 tsp. of salt and ½ tsp. of minced garlic. Stir to coat. Add peppers and onions to the Air Fryer basket with the potatoes. Cook for five minutes. Shake the basket and cook for an additional five minutes.

PER SERVING

Calories: 199 | Fat: 1 g | Carbs:43 g | Protein: 5 g| Fiber: 1g

Ezekiel Bread Toast

Prep time: 10 minutes | Cook time: 10 minutes |
Serves 2

- 4 ezekiel bread slices, cut diagonally in half
- 2 eggs
- ½ c. coconut milk
- 2 tbsp. coconut sugar
- 1 packet of stevia
- 1 tsp. vanilla
- 1 pinch cinnamon
- To serve:
- banana slices
- maple syrup
- berries

1. At 300°F, preheat your air fryer.
2. Beat eggs with coconut milk, coconut sugar, stevia, vanilla, and cinnamon in a shallow bowl.
3. Dip each bread slice in the egg-milk mixture.
4. Place the slices in the air fryer basket and air fry for 10 minutes.
5. Garnish and Serve.

PER SERVING

Calories: 390 | Fat: 20.6g | Carbs: 39.1g |
Protein: 14.2g | Fiber: 2g

Sweet Potato Veggie Hash

Prep time: 15 minutes | Cook time:28 minutes
|Serves 4

- 1 tbsp. olive oil
- 3 Yukon Gold potatoes, peeled and chopped
- 1 sweet potato, peeled and chopped
- 1 yellow onion, diced
- 1 red bell pepper, diced
- 2 garlic cloves, sliced
- 1 tsp. dried thyme
- ½ tsp. sea salt
- ⅛ tsp. freshly ground black pepper

1. In a medium bowl, toss the olive oil with the Yukon Gold and sweet potatoes. Place in the air fryer basket.
2. Set or preheat the air fryer to 400°F. Place the basket in the air fryer and cook the potatoes for 15 minutes, stirring every 5 minutes, until they are tender.
3. Add the onion, bell pepper, garlic, thyme, salt, and pepper to the basket and toss with the potatoes.
4. Bake for 8 to 13 minutes longer, stirring halfway through cooking time, until the potatoes are browned and crisp and the vegetables are crisp-tender. Serve.

PER SERVING

Calories: 176 | Protein: 4g | Fat: 4g |Carbs: 34g | Fiber: 4g

Vegetable Pita Sandwiches

Prep time: 15 minutes | Cook time: 9 to 12 minutes | Serves 4

- 1 baby eggplant, peeled and chopped
- 1 red bell pepper, sliced
- ½ cup diced red onion
- ½ cup shredded carrot
- 1 tsp. olive oil
- ⅓ cup low-fat Greek yogurt
- ½ tsp. dried tarragon
- 2 low-sodium whole-wheat pita breads, halved crosswise

1. In a 6-by-2-inch pan, stir together the eggplant, red bell pepper, red onion, carrot, and olive oil. Put the vegetable mixture into the air fryer basket and roast for 7 to 9 minutes, stirring once, until the vegetables are tender. Drain if necessary.
2. In a small bowl, thoroughly mix the yogurt and tarragon until well combined.
3. Stir the yogurt mixture into the vegetables. Stuff one-fourth of this mixture into each pita pocket.
4. Place the sandwiches in the air fryer and cook for 2 to 3 minutes, or until the bread is toasted. Serve immediately.

PER SERVING

Calories: 176| Fat: 4g |Protein: 7g|Carbs: 27g| Fiber: 3g

Cranberry Bread

Prep time: 15 minutes | Cook time: 30 minutes | Serves 10

- 4 eggs
- 3 cups flour
- 2/3 cups sugar
- 2/3 cup vegetable oil
- ½ cup milk
- 1 tsp. vanilla extract
- 2 tsp. baking powder
- 2 cups fresh cranberries

1. In a bowl, add all the ingredients (except the cranberries) and stir until well combined.
2. Gently fold in the cranberries.
3. Place the mixture into a lightly greased baking pan evenly. Select the "Air Fry" mode. Press the Time button and set the cooking time to thirty mins. Then push the Temp button and rotate the dial to set the temperature at 320° °F.
4. Press the Start button. When the unit beeps, open the lid.
5. Arrange the pan in the basket of the Air Fryer and insert it in the oven. Place the pan onto a wire rack and cook for about 10-15 mins.
6. Carefully invert the bread onto the wire rack to cool completely before slicing. Cut the bread into desired-sized slices.

PER SERVING

Calories: 436 | Fat: 16.9 g | Carbs:65.4 g |Protein: 13g| Fiber: 1g

French Toast with Flaxseed and Strawberries

Prep time: 15 minutes | Cook time: 10 minutes | Serves 4

- ¼ cup of brown sugar, cut in half
- ½ tsp. of cinnamon powder
- 2 eggs, beaten
- 1/4 tsp. of the essence of vanilla bean
- ¼ cup nonfat milk
- 4 pieces of whole-grain bread, cut into strips
- 2/3 of a cup of ground flax seeds
- Cooking spray
- ¼ tsp. of confectioner's sugar powder
- 1 ½ of cut strawberries

1. Add one tbsp. of brown sugar to a bowl.
2. Cinnamon, eggs, vanilla, and milk should be stirred in at this point.
3. Coat the bread strips with the mixture and set them aside.
4. Flax seed meal should be used for dredging, and oil should be sprayed on top.
5. 10 minutes in the air fryer at 375 °F, flipping once.
6. Place on a platter for serving.
7. Sugar powder should be sprinkled on top.
8. Strawberry preserves should be served on the side.
9. Serving suggestion: Honey or maple syrup, drizzled over the top.
10. Preparation and cooking tips: For this dish, use a loaf made with whole grains that is of good quality.

PER SERVING
Calories: 147 | Fat: 11g | Carbs: 3g | Protein: 9g | Fiber: 1g

Herb-Roasted Vegetables

Prep time: 10 minutes | Cook time: 14 to 18 minutes | Serves 4

- 1 red bell pepper, sliced
- 1 (8-ounce) package sliced mushrooms
- 1 cup green beans, cut into 2-inch pieces
- ⅓ cup diced red onion
- 3 garlic cloves, sliced
- 1 tsp. olive oil
- ½ tsp. dried basil
- ½ tsp. dried tarragon

1. In a medium bowl, mix the red bell pepper, mushrooms, green beans, red onion, and garlic. Drizzle with the olive oil. Toss to coat.
2. Add the herbs and toss again.
3. Place the vegetables in the air fryer basket. Roast for 14 to 18 minutes, or until tender. Serve immediately.

PER SERVING

Calories: 41|Fat: 1g |Protein: 2g|Carbs: 5g| Fiber: 2g

Spinach Frittata

Prep time: 5 minutes | Cook time: 8 minutes | Serves 1

- 3 eggs
- 1 cup spinach, chopped
- 1 small onion, minced
- 2 tbsp mozzarella cheese, grated
- Salt and Pepper

1. Preheat the Air Fryer to 350 °F. Spray a pan with cook spray.
2. In a bowl, whisk the eggs with the remaining ingredients until well combined.
3. Pour the egg mixture into the prepared pan and place it in the Air Fryer basket.
4. Cook frittata for eight mins.

PER SERVING

Calories: 384 | Fat: 23.3 g | Carbs:10.7 g | Protein: 6g| Fiber: 1g

Chapter 5

Poultry

Basil Chicken Bites

**Prep time: 10 minutes | Cook time: 30 minutes |
Serves 4**

- 1 1/2 lb. chicken breasts, skinless; boneless and cubed
- 1/2 cup chicken stock
- 2 tsp. smoked paprika
- Salt and pepper
- 1/2 tsp. basil; dried

1. In a pan that fits the Air Fryer, combine all the ingredients, toss, introduce the pan to the Air Fryer and cook at 390°F for 25 minutes.
2. Divide between plates and serve.

PER SERVING

Calories:21.2 | Fat: 12.2 g | Carbs: 4.5 g | Protein: 12.3 g | Fiber: 1g

Italian-Style Chicken Drumsticks

**Prep time: 25 minutes | Cook time:20 minutes
|Serves 4**

- 4 chicken drumsticks, bone-in
- 1 tbsp. butter
- 1/2 tsp. cayenne pepper
- 1 tsp. Italian herb mix
- Sea salt and ground black pepper, to taste

1. Pat the chicken drumsticks dry with paper towels. Toss the chicken drumsticks with the remaining ingredients.
2. Cook the chicken drumsticks at 370 °F for 20 minutes, turning them over halfway through the cooking time.
3. Bon appétit!

PER SERVING

Calories: 235 | Fat: 14.8g | Carbs: 0.3g | Protein: 23.2g | Fiber: 0.3g

Stuffed Turkey Roulade

Prep time: 10 minutes | Cook time: 45 minutes | Serves 4

- 1 (2-pound) boneless turkey breast, skin removed
- 1 tsp. salt
- ½ tsp. black pepper
- 4 ounces goat cheese
- 1 tbsp. fresh thyme
- 1 tbsp. fresh sage
- 2 garlic cloves, minced
- 2 tbsp. olive oil
- Fresh chopped parsley, for garnish

1. Preheat the air fryer to 380°F.
2. Using a sharp knife, butterfly the turkey breast, and season both sides with salt and pepper and set aside.
3. In a small bowl, mix together the goat cheese, thyme, sage, and garlic.
4. Spread the cheese mixture over the turkey breast, then roll it up tightly, tucking the ends underneath.
5. Place the turkey breast roulade onto a piece of aluminum foil, wrap it up, and place it into the air fryer.
6. Bake for 30 minutes. Remove the foil from the turkey breast and brush the top with oil, then continue cooking for another 10 to 15 minutes, or until the outside has browned and the internal temperature reaches 165°F.
7. Remove and cut into 1-inch-wide slices and serve with a sprinkle of parsley on top.

PER SERVING
Calories: 397 | Fat: 18g | Protein: 58g | Carbs: 1g | Fiber: 0g

Mediterranean-Style Chicken Fillets

Prep time: 15 minutes | Cook time:12 minutes |Serves 4

- 1 ½ pounds chicken fillets
- 1 tbsp. olive oil
- 1 tsp. garlic, minced
- 1 tbsp. Greek seasoning mix
- 1/2 tsp. red pepper flakes, crushed
- Sea salt and ground black pepper, to taste

1. Pat the chicken dry with paper towels. Toss the chicken with the remaining ingredients.
2. Cook the chicken fillets at 380 °F for 12 minutes, turning them over halfway through the cooking time.
3. Bon appétit!

PER SERVING

Calories: 227| Fat: 13.4g | Carbs: 0.2g | Protein: 23.4g | Fiber: 1g

Nutty Chicken Nuggets

Prep time: 10 minutes | Cook time: 10 to 13 minutes | Serves 4

- 1 egg white
- 1 tbsp. freshly squeezed lemon juice
- ½ tsp. dried basil
- ½ tsp. ground paprika
- 1 pound low-sodium boneless skinless chicken breasts, cut into 1½-inch cubes
- ½ cup ground almonds
- 2 slices low-sodium whole-wheat bread, crumbled

1. In a shallow bowl, beat the egg white, lemon juice, basil, and paprika with a fork until foamy.
2. Add the chicken and stir to coat.
3. On a plate, mix the almonds and bread crumbs.
4. Toss the chicken cubes in the almond and bread crumb mixture until coated.
5. Bake the nuggets in the air fryer, in two batches, for 10 to 13 minutes, or until the chicken reaches an internal temperature of 165°F on a meat thermometer. Serve immediately.

PER SERVING

Calories: 249|Fat: 8g |Protein: 32g|Carbs: 13g|Fiber: 3g

Greek-Inspired Turkey Burgers

Prep time: 5 minutes | Cook time: 10 minutes | Serves 4

- 1 pound ground turkey, 93% lean
- ½ cup low-sodium feta cheese
- 2 ounces diced kalamata olives
- 2 cups frozen spinach, thawed
- ½ cup chopped red onion
- 1 tbsp. dried oregano
- 1 tsp. granulated garlic
- ½ tsp. freshly ground black pepper

1. Preheat the air fryer to 375°F.
2. In a large bowl, stir together the turkey, feta cheese, olives, spinach, onion, oregano, garlic, and black pepper. with wet hands, form the mixture into 4 patties.
3. Working in batches if necessary, place the burgers in a single layer in the air fryer basket. Cook for 6 minutes, then flip them over and cook for another 6 minutes, or until the internal temperature reaches 165°F.

PER SERVING

Calories: 280 |Fat: 9g | Carbs: 9g | Fiber: 3g | Protein: 43g

Greek Chicken Kebabs

Prep time: 15 minutes | Cook time: 15 minutes | Serves 4

- 3 tbsp. freshly squeezed lemon juice
- 2 tsp. olive oil
- 2 tbsp. chopped fresh flat-leaf parsley
- ½ tsp. dried oregano
- ½ tsp. dried mint
- 1 pound low-sodium boneless skinless chicken breasts, cut into 1-inch pieces
- 1 cup cherry tomatoes
- 1 small yellow summer squash, cut into 1-inch cubes

1. In a large bowl, whisk the lemon juice, olive oil, parsley, oregano, and mint.
2. Add the chicken and stir to coat. Let stand for 10 minutes at room temperature.
3. Alternating the items, thread the chicken, tomatoes, and squash onto 8 bamboo (see Tip, here) or metal skewers that fit in an air fryer. Brush with marinade.
4. Grill the kebabs for about 15 minutes, brushing once with any remaining marinade, until the chicken reaches an internal temperature of 165°F on a meat thermometer. Discard any remaining marinade. Serve immediately.

PER SERVING

Calories: 163|Fat: 4g|Protein: 27g|Carbs: 4g| Fiber: 1g

Herbed Roasted Chicken

Prep time: 15 minutes | Cook time: 1 hour | Serves 7

- 3 garlic cloves, minced
- 1 (5-pounds) whole chicken
- 1 tsp. fresh lemon zest, finely grated
- 1 tsp. dried thyme, crushed
- 1 tsp. dried oregano, crushed
- 1 tsp. dried rosemary, crushed
- 1 tsp. smoked paprika
- 2 tbsp. fresh lemon juice
- 2 tbsp. olive oil
- Salt and ground black pepper

1. In a bowl, mix the garlic, lemon zest, herbs, and spices.
2. Rub the chicken evenly with the herb mixture.
3. Drizzle the chicken with lemon juice and oil. Set aside at room temperature for about 2 hours.
4. Set the temperature of the Air Fryer to 360 °F. Grease the Air Fryer basket.
5. Place chicken into the prepared Air Fryer basket, breast side down. Air Fry for about 50 minutes.
6. Flip the chicken and Air Fry for about 10 more minutes.
7. Remove from the Air Fryer and place chicken onto a cutting board for about 10 minutes before carving.

PER SERVING

Calories: 861 | Carbs:1.4 g | Protein: 72.1 g | Fat: 45 g | Fiber: 2g

Turkey Meatballs

Prep time: 10 Minutes | Cook time: 20 minutes | Serves 6

- 1 lb ground turkey
- 2 eggs, lightly beaten
- 1 tbsp. basil, chopped
- 1/3 cup coconut flour
- 1 tbsp. dried onion flakes
- 2 cups zucchini, grated
- 1 tsp. dried oregano
- 1 tbsp. garlic, minced
- 1 tsp. cumin
- 1 tbsp. nutritional yeast
- Salt and Pepper

1. Select "Bake" to your Air Fryer and preheat to 390 °F for twenty minutes.
2. Add all ingredients into a bowl and mix until well combined.
3. Make small balls from the meat mixture, place them on a roasting pan and bake for twenty minutes.

PER SERVING

Calories: 213 | Fat: 11.7 g | Carbs:7.9 g | Protein: 23.9 g | Fiber: 1.3g

Lentil Chicken Soup

Prep time: 15 minutes | Cook time: 2 hrs. 26 minutes | Serves 4

- ½ lb. boneless chicken breasts
- 2 tbsp. olive oil
- 1 medium yellow onion, chopped
- 4 garlic cloves, minced
- 1 medium yellow bell pepper, chopped
- 1 medium red bell pepper, chopped
- 2 cup red lentils, rinsed
- 2 cup water
- 1 tsp. cumin ground
- ¾ tsp. black pepper
- 2 cup low-sodium vegetable broth
- ½ cup cilantro, chopped
- 2 limes, juiced

1. Rub chicken with 1 tbsp oil and place it in the air fryer basket,
2. Air fry the chicken for 20 minutes and flip once cooked halfway through.
3. Shred the cooked chicken once cooled, and then keep it aside.
4. Sauté onions with peppers and oil in a large skillet for 5 minutes on medium-high heat.
5. Stir in garlic and sauté for 1 minute.
6. Transfer this mixture to a slow cooker and add red lentils, water, chicken, broth, lime juice, black pepper, and cumin; then cover and cook for 4 hours on low heat or 2 hours on high heat.
7. Garnish with cilantro and serve.

PER SERVING

Calories: 410 | Fat: 4.7g | Carbs: 64.8g | Protein: 27.6g | Fiber: 1g

Chapter 6

Meats

Mediterranean Filet Mignon

Prep time: 15 minutes | Cook time:14 minutes |Serves 4

- 1 ½ pounds filet mignon
- Sea salt and ground black pepper, to taste
- 2 tbsp. olive oil
- 1 tsp. dried rosemary
- 1 tsp. dried thyme
- 1 tsp. dried basil
- 2 cloves garlic, minced

1. Toss the beef with the remaining ingredients | place the beef in the Air Fryer cooking basket.
2. Cook the beef at 400 °F for 14 minutes, turning it over halfway through the cooking time.
3. Enjoy!

PER SERVING

Calories: 385 | Fat: 26g | Carbs: 2.2g | Protein: 36.2g | Fiber: 0.3g

Herb and Onion Beef Roast

Prep time: 55 minutes | Cook time:45 minutes |Serves 4

- 1 ½ pounds beef eye round roast
- 1 tbsp. olive oil
- Sea salt and ground black pepper, to taste
- 1 onion, sliced
- 1 rosemary sprig
- 1 thyme sprig

1. Toss the beef with the olive oil, salt, and black pepper; place the beef in the Air Fryer cooking basket.
2. Cook the beef eye round roast at 390 °F for 45 minutes, turning it over halfway through the cooking time.
3. Top the beef with the onion, rosemary, and thyme. Continue to cook an additional 10 minutes.
4. Enjoy!

PER SERVING

Calories: 268 |Fat: 13.6g |Carbs: 1.2g | Protein: 35.2g | Fiber: 0.2g

Greek Vegetable Skillet

Prep time: 10 minutes | Cook time: 9 to 19 minutes | Serves 4

- ½ pound 96 percent lean ground beef
- 2 medium tomatoes, chopped
- 1 onion, chopped
- 2 garlic cloves, minced
- 2 cups fresh baby spinach
- 2 tbsp. freshly squeezed lemon juice
- ⅓ cup low-sodium beef broth
- 2 tbsp. crumbled low-sodium feta cheese

1. In a 6-by-2-inch metal pan, crumble the beef. Cook in the air fryer for 3 to 7 minutes, stirring once during cooking, until browned. Drain off any fat or liquid.
2. Add the tomatoes, onion, and garlic to the pan. Air-fry for 4 to 8 minutes more, or until the onion is tender.
3. Add the spinach, lemon juice, and beef broth. Air-fry for 2 to 4 minutes more, or until the spinach is wilted.
4. Sprinkle with the feta cheese and serve immediately.

PER SERVING

Calories: 97|Fat: 1g |Protein: 15g|Carbs: 5g| Fiber: 1g

Italian Pulled Pork Ragu

Prep time: 70 minutes | Cook time:70 minutes |Serves 5

- 2 pounds beef shoulder
- Kosher salt and ground black pepper, to taste
- 2 garlic cloves, minced
- 1 tbsp. Italian seasoning mix

1. Toss the beef shoulder with the remaining ingredients | now, place the beef shoulder in the Air Fryer cooking basket.
2. Cook the beef shoulder at 390 °F for 15 minutes, turn the beef shoulder over and reduce the temperature to 360 °F.
3. Continue to cook the beef shoulder for approximately 55 minutes or until cooked through.
4. Shred the beef shoulder with two forks and serve with toppings of choice. Bon appétit!

PER SERVING

Calories: 259 | Fat: 10.9g | Carbs: 2.5g | Protein: 37g | Fiber: 0.4g

Greek Pulled Beef

Prep time: 70 minutes | Cook time:70 minutes |Serves 4

- 1½ pounds beef brisket
- 2 tbsp. olive oil
- Sea salt and freshly ground black pepper, to season
- 1 tsp. dried oregano
- 1 tsp. mustard powder
- 1/2 tsp. ground cumin
- 2 cloves garlic, minced
- 2 tbsp. chives, chopped
- 2 tbsp. cilantro, chopped

1. Toss the beef brisket with the rest of the ingredients; now, place the beef brisket in the Air Fryer cooking basket.
2. Cook the beef brisket at 390 °F for 15 minutes, turn the beef over and reduce the temperature to 360 °F.
3. Continue to cook the beef brisket for approximately 55 minutes or until cooked through.
4. Shred the beef with two forks and serve with toppings of choice. Bon appétit!

PER SERVING

Calories: 402| Fat: 32.2g | Carbs: 1.2g | Protein: 25.2g | Fiber: 0.3g

Mushroom and Beef Patties

Prep time: 15 minutes | Cook time:15 minutes |Serves 4

- 1 pound ground chuck
- 2 garlic cloves, minced
- 1 small onion, chopped
- 1 cup mushrooms, chopped
- 1 tsp. cayenne pepper
- Sea salt and ground black pepper, to taste
- 4 brioche rolls

1. Mix the ground chuck, garlic, onion, mushrooms, cayenne pepper, salt, and black pepper until everything is well combined. Form the mixture into four patties.
2. Cook the patties at 380 °F for about 15 minutes or until cooked through; make sure to turn them over halfway through the cooking time.
3. Serve your patties on the prepared brioche rolls and enjoy!

PER SERVING

Calories: 305 | Fat: 10.4g | Carbs: 25.3g | Protein: 27.7g | Fiber: 1.7g

talian-Style Burgers

Prep time: 20 minutes | Cook time:15 minutes
|Serves 4

- 1 pound ground pork
- Sea salt and ground black pepper, to taste
- 1 tbsp. Italian herb mix
- 1 small onion, chopped
- 1 tsp. garlic, minced
- 1/4 cup parmesan cheese, grated
- 1/4 cup seasoned breadcrumbs
- 1 egg
- 4 hamburger buns
- 4 tsp. Dijon mustard
- 4 tbsp. mayonnaise

1. In a mixing bowl, thoroughly combine the pork, spices, onion, garlic, parmesan, breadcrumbs, and egg. Form the mixture into four patties.
2. Cook the burgers at 380 °F for about 15 minutes or until cooked through; make sure to turn them over halfway through the cooking time.
3. Serve your burgers with hamburger buns, mustard, and mayonnaise. Enjoy!

PER SERVING

Calories: 593 | Fat: 38.9g |Carbs: 30.2g
|Protein: 27.6g | Fiber: 2.7g

Herb Filet Mignon

Prep time: 20 minutes | Cook time:14 minutes
|Serves 4

- 1 ½ pounds filet mignon
- 2 tbsp. olive oil
- 2 cloves garlic, pressed
- 1 tbsp. Italian herb mix
- 1 tsp. cayenne pepper
- Kosher salt and freshly ground black pepper, to taste

1. Toss the beef with the remaining ingredients | place the beef in the Air Fryer cooking basket.
2. Cook the beef at 400 °F for 14 minutes, turning it over halfway through the cooking time.
3. Enjoy!

PER SERVING

Calories: 300 | Fat: 17.4g | Carbs: 0.7g |
Protein: 35.3g | Fiber: 0.2g

Beef Brisket Stew

Prep time: 15 minutes | Cook time: 1 hour 6 mins. | Serves 6

- 1 tbsp. olive oil
- 2 ½ lbs. lean beef brisket, cut into cubes
- black pepper, to taste
- 1 ½ c. onions, chopped
- 4 garlic cloves, smashed and peeled
- 1 tsp. dried thyme
- 1 can (14.5 oz.) of no-salt-added tomatoes and liquid
- ¼ c. red wine vinegar
- 1 c. low-sodium beef stock

1. At 350°F, preheat your air fryer.
2. Rub one tbsp. of oil over the brisket while seasoning it with black pepper.
3. Air fry the brisket for 30 minutes.
4. Add onions to the Dutch oven, then cook for 5 minutes.
5. Stir in thyme and garlic, then cook for 1 minute.
6. Add tomatoes, beef, vinegar, and stock, then cover and cook for 30 minutes.
7. Serve warm.

PER SERVING

Calories: 428 | Fat: 14.2g | Carbs: 6.3g | Protein: 58.2g | Fiber: 2g

Greek Pork Gyros

Prep time: 55 minutes | Cook time:55 minutes |Serves 4

- 1 pound pork shoulder
- 1 tsp. smoked paprika
- 1/2 tsp. onion powder
- 1 tsp. garlic powder
- 1/2 tsp. ground cumin
- 1/2 tsp. ground bay leaf
- Sea salt and ground black pepper, to taste
- 4 pitta bread, warmed

1. Toss the pork on all sides, top and bottom, with the spices. Place the pork in a lightly greased Air Fryer cooking basket.
2. Cook the pork at 360 °F for 55 minutes, turning it over halfway through the cooking time.
3. Shred the pork with two forks and serve on warmed pitta bread and some extra toppings of choice. Enjoy!

PER SERVING

Calories: 479 | Fat: 20.9g |Carbs: 35.7g | Protein: 34.4g |Fiber: 1.9g

Chapter 7

Seafood

Asian Fish Fillet

Prep time: 10 minutes | Cook time: 10 minutes | Serves 2

- 2 halibut fish fillets
- 1 tbsp oyster sauce
- 1/2 tbsp lemon juice
- 1 tbsp brown sugar
- 1 tsp tamari sauce
- 2 tsp fish sauce
- 1 tsp ginger garlic paste
- Pepper
- Salt

1. Preheat your air fryer to 400 °F.
2. Mix fish sauce, tamari sauce, lemon juice, ginger garlic paste, oyster sauce, and brown sugar in a small bowl.
3. Brush fish fillets with fish sauce mixture
4. Place fish fillets into the air fryer basket and cook for 10 minutes.
5. Serve and enjoy.

PER SERVING

Calories: 225 | Fat: 4.5 g | Carbs: 6.7 g | Protein: 37.1 g | Fiber: 2g

Chipotle Spiced Shrimp

Prep time: 10 minutes | Cook time: 5 minutes | Serves 2

- 1 lb. uncooked shrimp, peeled and deveined
- 2 tbsp. low-sodium tomato paste
- 1 ½ tsp. Water
- ½ tsp. Olive oil
- ½ tsp. Minced garlic
- ½ tsp. Chipotle chili powder
- ½ tsp. chopped fresh oregano

1. Mix tomato paste, oil, water, chili powder, oregano, and garlic.
2. Toss in shrimp, mix well to coat, cover and refrigerate for 5 minutes.
3. At 300°F, preheat your air fryer and grease it with cooking spray.
4. Air fry the shrimp for 5 minutes.
5. Serve.

PER SERVING

Calories: 295 | Fat: 5.1g | Carbs: 6.9g | Protein: 52.4g |Fiber: 2g

Sea Bass with Roasted Root Vegetables

Prep time: 10 minutes | Cook time: 15 minutes | Serves 4

- 1 carrot, diced small
- 1 parsnip, diced small
- 1 rutabaga, diced small
- ¼ cup olive oil
- 2 tsp. salt, divided
- 4 sea bass fillets
- ½ tsp. onion powder
- 2 garlic cloves, minced
- 1 lemon, sliced, plus additional wedges for serving

1. Preheat the air fryer to 380°F.
2. In a small bowl, toss the carrot, parsnip, and rutabaga with olive oil and 1 tsp. salt.
3. Lightly season the sea bass with the remaining 1 tsp. of salt and the onion powder, then place it into the air fryer basket in a single layer.
4. Spread the garlic over the top of each fillet, then cover with lemon slices.
5. Pour the prepared vegetables into the basket around and on top of the fish. Roast for 15 minutes.
6. Serve with additional lemon wedges if desired.

PER SERVING

Calories: 299 | Fat: 16g | Protein: 25g | Carbs: 13g | Fiber: 3g

Greek Fish Pita

Prep time: 15 minutes | Cook time:35 minutes |Serves 4

- 1 pound monkfish fillets
- 1 tbsp. olive oil
- Sea salt and ground black pepper, to taste
- Sea salt and ground black pepper, to taste
- 1 tsp. cayenne pepper
- 4 tbsp. coleslaw
- 1 avocado, pitted, peeled and diced
- 1 tbsp. fresh parsley, chopped
- 4 (6-1/2 inch) Greek pitas, warmed

1. Toss the fish fillets with the olive oil; place them in a lightly oiled Air Fryer cooking basket.
2. Cook the fish fillets at 400 °F for about 14 minutes, turning them over halfway through the cooking time.
3. Assemble your pitas with the chopped fish and remaining ingredients and serve warm. Bon appétit!

PER SERVING

Calories: 494 | Fat: 24.3g | Carbs: 43.8g | Protein: 28.8g | Fiber: 8.3g

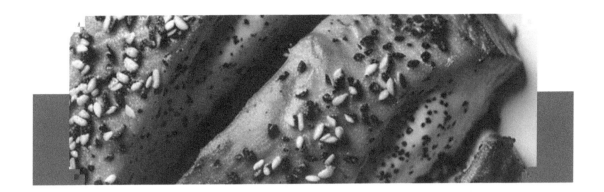

Crusted Salmon with Kale Chips

Prep time: 10 minutes | Cook time: 15 minutes | Serves 4

- 1 pound skinless salmon fillets, cut into 4-inch fillets
- 2 tbsp. everything bagel seasoning, plus 1 tsp.
- extra-virgin olive oil cooking spray
- 1 bunch fresh curly kale (about 6 ounces), stemmed, leaves torn into 2-inch pieces
- 2 tbsp. extra-virgin olive oil

1. Preheat the air fryer to 350°F.
2. Place the salmon on a plate or flat surface and sprinkle with 2 tbsp. of everything bagel seasoning, firmly pressing the seasoning into the fish.
3. Working in batches if necessary, mist the air fryer basket with the olive oil. Arrange the salmon fillets in a single layer in the air fryer basket, seasoned-side up. Mist with the olive oil cooking spray and cook for 6 to 10 minutes, depending on thickness. The salmon is done when the internal temperature reaches 145°F.
4. While the salmon is cooking, in a medium bowl, massage the kale with the olive oil. Sprinkle with the remaining 1 tsp. of everything bagel seasoning.
5. Place the kale in the air fryer, set the temperature to 375°F, and cook for 3 minutes, shaking and misting with more oil halfway through the cooking time, until the kale is crispy.

PER SERVING
Calories: 251 |Fat: 16g | Carbs: 2g | Fiber: 2g | Protein: 26g

Salmon Nachos

Prep time: 10 minutes | Cook time: 9 to 12 minutes | Serves 6

- 2 ounces (about 36) baked no-salt corn tortilla chips
- 1 (5-ounce) baked salmon fillet, flaked
- ½ cup canned low-sodium black beans, rinsed and drained
- 1 red bell pepper, chopped
- ½ cup grated carrot
- 1 jalapeño pepper, minced
- ⅓ cup shredded low-sodium low-fat Swiss cheese
- 1 tomato, chopped

1. In a 6-by-2-inch pan, layer the tortilla chips. Top with the salmon, black beans, red bell pepper, carrot, jalapeño, and Swiss cheese.
2. Bake in the air fryer for 9 to 12 minutes, or until the cheese is melted and starts to brown.
3. Top with the tomato and serve.

PER SERVING

Calories: 127|Fat: 2g|Protein: 9g|Carbs: 19g| Fiber: 5g

Cheesy Italian Squid

Prep time: 10 minutes | Cook time:5 minutes |Serves 4

- 1 ½ pounds small squid tubes
- 2 tbsp. butter, melted
- 1 chili pepper, chopped
- 2 garlic cloves, minced
- 1 tsp. red pepper flakes
- Sea salt and ground black pepper, to taste
- 1/4 cup dry white wine
- 2 tbsp. fresh lemon juice
- 1 tsp. Mediterranean herb mix
- 2 tbsp. Parmigiano-Reggiano cheese, grated

1. Toss all ingredients , except for the Parmigiano-Reggiano cheese, in a lightly greased Air Fryer cooking basket.
2. Cook your squid at 400 °F for 5 minutes, tossing the basket halfway through the cooking time.
3. Top the warm squid with the cheese. Bon appétit!

PER SERVING

Calories: 267 | Fat: 11.3g | Carbs: 9.3g | Protein: 29.8g | Fiber: 0.4g

Baked Grouper with Tomatoes and Garlic

Prep time: 5 minutes | Cook time: 12 minutes | Serves 4

- 4 grouper fillets
- ½ tsp. salt
- 3 garlic cloves, minced
- 1 tomato, sliced
- ¼ cup sliced Kalamata olives
- ¼ cup fresh dill, roughly chopped
- Juice of 1 lemon
- ¼ cup olive oil

1. Preheat the air fryer to 380°F.
2. Season the grouper fillets on all sides with salt, then place into the air fryer basket and top with the minced garlic, tomato slices, olives, and fresh dill.
3. Drizzle the lemon juice and olive oil over the top of the grouper, then bake for 10 to 12 minutes, or until the internal temperature reaches 145°F.

PER SERVING

Calories: 271 | Fat: 16g | Protein: 28g | Carbs: 3g | Fiber: 1g

Salmon Spring Rolls

Prep time: 20 minutes | Cook time: 8 to 10 minutes | Serves 4

- ½ pound salmon fillet
- 1 tsp. toasted sesame oil
- 1 onion, sliced
- 8 rice paper wrappers
- 1 yellow bell pepper, thinly sliced
- 1 carrot, shredded
- ⅓ cup chopped fresh flat-leaf parsley
- ¼ cup chopped fresh basil

1. Put the salmon in the air fryer basket and drizzle with the sesame oil. Add the onion. Air-fry for 8 to 10 minutes, or until the salmon just flakes when tested with a fork and the onion is tender.
2. Meanwhile, fill a small shallow bowl with warm water. One at a time, dip the rice paper wrappers into the water and place on a work surface.
3. Top each wrapper with one-eighth each of the salmon and onion mixture, yellow bell pepper, carrot, parsley, and basil. Roll up the wrapper, folding in the sides, to enclose the ingredients.
4. If you like, bake in the air fryer at 380°F for 7 to 9 minutes, until the rolls are crunchy. Cut the rolls in half to serve.

PER SERVING

Calories: 95|Fat: 2g | Protein: 13g|Carbs: 8g| Fiber: 2g

Parmesan Shrimp

Prep time: 5 minutes | Cook time:10 minutes | Serves 4

- 2 tbsp. olive oil
- 8 cups, peeled, deveined, jumbo cooked shrimp
- 2/3 cup (grated) parmesan cheese
- 1 tsp. onion powder
- 1 tsp. pepper
- 4 cloves of minced garlic
- 1/2 tsp. oregano
- 1 tsp. basil
- Lemon wedges

1. Mix parmesan cheese, onion powder, oregano, olive oil, garlic, basil, and pepper in a bowl. Coat the shrimp in this mixture.
2. Spray oil on the Air Fryer basket and put shrimp in it. Cook for ten minutes at 350°F.
3. Drizzle the lemon on the shrimp before serving.

PER SERVING

Calories: 199 | Fat: 12.3 g | Carbs: 5.5 g | Protein: 11.7 g | Fiber: 3g`

Basil-Parmesan Crusted Salmon

Prep time: 5 minutes | Cook time:15 minutes | Serves 4

- 3 tbsp. grated parmesan
- skinless four salmon fillets
- 1/4 tsp. salt
- freshly ground black pepper
- 3 tbsp. low- fat mayonnaise
- basil leaves, chopped
- half lemon

1. Let the Air Fryer preheat to 400 °F. Spray the basket with olive oil.
2. Season the salmon with pepper, salt, and lemon juice.
3. Mix two tbsp. of Parmesan cheese in a bowl with mayonnaise and basil leaves.
4. Add this mix and the rest of the Parmesan on top of the salmon and cook for seven minutes.

PER SERVING

Calories:288 | Carbs: 1.45 g | Protein: 30.6 g | Fat: 17.5 g| Fiber: 1g

Chapter 8

Vegan and Vegetarian

Vegan Cauliflower Rice

Prep time: 10 minutes | Cook time: 20 minutes | Serves 3

- 2 carrots, diced
- ½ cup onion, diced
- 2 tbsp. soy sauce
- ½ block firm tofu, crumbled
- 1 tsp. turmeric

For the rice:

- 3 cups riced cauliflower
- 2 tbsp. sodium soy sauce, reduced
- ½ cup broccoli, finely chopped
- 1 tbsp. rice vinegar
- ½ cup peas, frozen
- 2 garlic cloves, minced
- 1 and ½ tsp. sesame oil, toasted
- 1 tbsp. ginger, minced
- 1 tbsp. rice vinegar
- ½ cup frozen peas

1. Preheat and set the Air Fryer's temperature to 370 °F.
2. Take a large bowl and add tofu, carrots, onion, soy sauce, and turmeric. Stir well to combine. Set the Air Fryer to cook for 10 minutes.
3. Take another bowl and add the remaining ingredients. Stir them well. Transfer into the Air Fryer and cook for 10 minutes more.

PER SERVING

Calories:152.3 | Fat: 4.1 g | Carbs: 17.8 g | Protein: 4 g | Fiber: 2g

Radish Couscous Salad

Prep time: 5 minutes | Cook time: 5 minutes | Serves 2

- 2 tbsp. lime juice
- 2 tsp. distilled white vinegar
- 2 tsp. ground cumin
- 2 cup couscous, cooked
- 1 cup chickpeas, cooked
- 1 cup fresh parsley, chopped
- ⅔ cup pomegranate seeds
- ½ cup radishes, sliced
- 2 cup baby spinach

1. At 300°F, preheat your air fryer.
2. Spread the chickpeas in the air fryer basket and air fry for 5 minutes.
3. Mix cumin, vinegar, and lime juice in a salad bowl.
4. Toss in couscous, chickpeas, parsley, pomegranate seeds, and radishes.
5. Mix the veggies with the dressing well.
6. Spread spinach on a platter and add the remaining salad on top.
7. Serve.

PER SERVING

Calories: 193 | Fat: 1.7g | Carbs: 37.6g | Protein: 8g | Fiber: 1.5g

Crispy Garlic Sliced Eggplant

Prep time: 5 minutes | Cook time: 25 minutes | Serves 4

- 1 egg
- 1 tbsp. water
- ½ cup whole wheat bread crumbs
- 1 tsp. garlic powder
- ½ tsp. dried oregano
- ½ tsp. salt
- ½ tsp. paprika
- 1 medium eggplant, sliced into ¼-inch-thick rounds
- 1 tbsp. olive oil

1. Preheat the air fryer to 360°F.
2. In a medium shallow bowl, beat together the egg and water until frothy.
3. In a separate medium shallow bowl, mix together bread crumbs, garlic powder, oregano, salt, and paprika.
4. Dip each eggplant slice into the egg mixture, then into the bread crumb mixture, coating the outside with crumbs. Place the slices in a single layer in the bottom of the air fryer basket.
5. Drizzle the tops of the eggplant slices with the olive oil, then fry for 15 minutes. Turn each slice and cook for an additional 10 minutes.

PER SERVING

Calories: 137 | Fat: 5g | Protein: 5g | Carbs: 19g | Fiber: 5g

Roasted Vegetable Salad

Prep time: 15 minutes | Cook time:11 minutes |Serves 4

- 1 yellow summer squash, sliced
- 1½ cups (2-inch pieces) fresh asparagus
- 1 orange bell pepper, sliced
- 1 cup sliced mushrooms
- 4 tbsp. olive oil, divided
- ½ tsp. sea salt
- 2 tbsp. freshly squeezed lemon juice
- 1 tbsp. freshly squeezed orange juice
- 1 tbsp. honey mustard
- 1 tsp. dried thyme

1. Put the squash, asparagus, bell pepper, and mushrooms in the air fryer basket and toss to mix. Drizzle the vegetables with 1 tbsp of olive oil and sprinkle with the salt. Put the basket in the air fryer.
2. Set or preheat the air fryer to 375°F. Roast for 8 to 11 minutes, tossing halfway through cooking time, until the vegetables are tender.
3. Meanwhile, in a large serving bowl whisk together the remaining 3 tbsp. of olive oil, lemon juice, orange juice, mustard, and thyme.
4. When the vegetables are done, add them to the serving bowl and toss to coat with the dressing. Serve immediately, at room temperature, or chill for a few hours before serving.

PER SERVING

Calories: 163 | Protein: 3g | Fat: 14g | Carbs: 9g | Fiber: 2g

Indian Spiced Okra
Prep time: 5 minutes | Cook time:20 minutes |Serves 4

- ½ pound okra (3 cups)
- 1 tbsp. coconut oil, melted
- 1 tsp. cumin
- 1 tsp. coriander
- 1 tsp. garlic granules
- ¼ tsp. sea salt
- ¼ tsp. turmeric
- ⅛ tsp. cayenne
- 1 tsp. fresh lime juice

1. Place the okra in a medium bowl and toss with the oil. Add the cumin, coriander, garlic, salt, turmeric, and cayenne. Stir well, preferably with a rubber spatula, until the okra is well coated with the seasonings.
2. Put the okra in the air fryer basket and fry for 7 minutes. Set the seasoning bowl aside. Remove the air fryer basket, stir or toss to evenly cook the okra, and place it back in the air fryer, frying for another 7 minutes. Remove the basket, toss, and check for doneness. At this point, you'll most likely need to fry your okra for another 6 minutes, but it depends on the size of your okra (smaller pieces cook more quickly). Remove when the pieces feel crisp, rather than "squishy." If you have a variety of sizes in your okra, you may need to remove smaller pieces, as they'll finish cooking before larger pieces.
3. Once all of the okra is crisp, place it back into the seasoning bowl. Sprinkle the lime juice on top, give the okra one last stir, and serve immediately.

PER SERVING
Calories: 58 | Fat: 4g | Carbs: 6g | Fiber: 2g | Protein: 1g

Vegetarian Chilli with Tofu

Prep time: 15 minutes | Cook time: 31 minutes | Serves 4

- 1 tbsp. olive oil
- 1 small yellow onion, chopped
- 12 oz. extra-firm tofu, cut into small pieces
- 2 cans (14 oz.) of diced tomatoes with no salt
- 1 can (14 oz.) of kidney beans with no salt, rinsed and drained
- 1 can (14 oz.) of black beans with no salt, rinsed and drained
- 3 tbsp. chili powder
- 1 tbsp. oregano
- 1 tbsp. chopped fresh cilantro

1. At 350°F, preheat your air fryer.
2. Spread tofu cubes in the air fryer basket and spray them with cooking spray.
3. Air fry the tofu for 10 minutes until golden brown.
4. Sauté onions with oil in a soup pot for 6 minutes.
5. Stir in oregano, chili powder, beans, and tomatoes, then cook to a boil.
6. Reduce the heat, cover, and cook on a simmer for 15 minutes.
7. Stir in tofu and mix evenly.
8. Garnish with cilantro and serve warm.

PER SERVING

Calories: 264 | Fat: 10g | Carbs: 30.4g | Protein: 17.6g | Fiber: 1g

Mediterranean-Style Veggies

Prep time: 15 minutes | Cook time:20 minutes |Serves 4

- 1½ cups cherry tomatoes
- 1 yellow bell pepper, sliced
- 1 small zucchini, sliced
- 1½ cups button mushrooms, halved lengthwise
- 2 tbsp. olive oil
- 1 tsp. dried basil
- ½ tsp. dried oregano
- ½ tsp. dried thyme
- ½ tsp. garlic powder
- ½ tsp. sea salt
- ⅛ tsp. freshly ground black pepper

1. Put the tomatoes, bell pepper, zucchini, and mushrooms in the air fryer basket. Drizzle with the olive oil and toss to coat. Then sprinkle with the basil, oregano, thyme, garlic powder, salt, and pepper and toss again. Put the basket in the air fryer.
2. Set or preheat the air fryer to 375°F and roast for 15 to 20 minutes, tossing twice during cooking time, until the vegetables are tender. Serve.

PER SERVING

Calories: 142 | Protein: 6g | Fat: 8g | Carbs: 17g | Fiber: 5g

Chapter 9

Snacks and Sides

Zucchini Parmesan Chips

Prep time: 10 minutes | Cook time: 20 minutes | Serves 6

- ½ cup seasoned, whole wheat breadcrumbs
- thinly slices of 2 zucchinis
- ½ cup (grated) parmesan cheese
- 1 egg whisked
- salt and pepper to taste

1. In a bowl, whisk the egg with a few tsp. of water, salt, and pepper.
2. In another bowl, mix the grated cheese and breadcrumbs.
3. Coat zucchini slices in the egg mixture, then in breadcrumbs. Put all in the rack and spray with olive oil.
4. Place the chips in the Air Fryer in a single layer, and cook for 8 minutes at 350 °F.

PER SERVING

Calories: 101.3 | Fat: 7.8 g | Carbs: 5.6 g | Protein: 11 g | Fiber: 2g

Mediterranean Potato Chips

Prep time: 20 minutes | Cook time:16 minutes |Serves 3

- 2 large-sized potatoes, thinly sliced
- 2 tbsp. olive oil
- 1 tsp. Mediterranean herb mix
- 1 tsp. cayenne pepper
- Coarse sea salt and ground black pepper, to taste

1. Start by preheating your Air Fryer to 360 °F.
2. Toss the potatoes with the remaining ingredients and place them in the Air Fryer cooking basket.
3. Air fry the potato chips for 16 minutes, shaking the basket halfway through the cooking time and working in batches.
4. Enjoy!

PER SERVING

Calories: 262 | Fat: 9.2g | Carbs: 42.1g | Protein: 4.9g | Fiber: 5.4g

Cozy Apple Crisp

Prep time: 10 minutes | Cook time:30 minutes |Serves 4

- 2 tbsp. coconut oil
- ¼ cup plus 2 tbsp. whole-wheat pastry flour (or gluten-free all-purpose flour)
- ¼ cup coconut sugar
- ⅛ tsp. sea salt
- 2 cups finely chopped (or thinly sliced) apples (no need to peel)
- 3 tbsp. water
- ½ tbsp. lemon juice
- ¾ tsp. cinnamon

1. In a 6-inch round, 2-inch deep baking pan, stir the apples with the water, lemon juice, and cinnamon until well combined.
2. Crumble the chilled topping over the apples. Bake for 30 minutes, or until the apples are tender and the crumble is crunchy and nicely browned. Serve immediately on its own or topped with nondairy milk, vegan ice cream, or nondairy whipped cream.

PER SERVING

Calories: 172 | Fat: 7g | Carbs: 29g | Fiber: 4g | Protein: 1g

Nutritious Roasted Chickpeas

Prep time: 10 minutes |Cook time: 14 minutes |Serves 2

- 14 oz can chickpeas, drained & rinsed
- 1 tsp dried oregano
- 1 tsp dried thyme
- 1 tsp dried rosemary
- 2 tbsp sesame oil
- 1 ½ tsp onion powder
- pepper
- salt

1. In a mixing bowl, toss chickpeas with oil, onion powder, rosemary, thyme, oregano, pepper, and salt until well coated.
2. Transfer chickpeas into the air fryer basket and cook at 370 °F for 14 minutes. Stir halfway through.
3. Serve and enjoy.

PER SERVING:

Calories: 369| Fat: 16.5g| Carbs: 47.6g| Protein: 10.3g | Fiber: 2g

Simple Berry Crisp

Prep time: 10 minutes | Cook time: 15 minutes | Serves 4

- 4 cups wild blueberries, fresh or frozen
- 1 tbsp. freshly squeezed lemon juice
- 1 tbsp. arrowroot flour or cornstarch
- 2 cups old-fashioned rolled oats
- ½ cup unsweetened applesauce
- ½ cup slivered almonds
- 1 tsp. pure vanilla extract
- 2 tbsp. ground cinnamon
- ¼ tsp. sea salt

1. Preheat the air fryer to 350°F.
2. In an air fryer baking pan, spread out the blueberries, top with the lemon juice, and sprinkle with the arrowroot flour.
3. In a large bowl, stir together the oats, applesauce, almonds, vanilla, cinnamon, and salt until combined.
4. Scatter the topping over the blueberries, ensuring the blueberries are completely covered.
5. Place the pan in the air fryer basket and cook for 15 minutes, until the blueberries are bubbling and the top is golden brown.

PER SERVING

Calories: 325 | Fat: 11g | Carbs: 54g | Fiber: 11g | Protein: 9g

Dill Beet Chips

Prep time: 10 minutes | Cook time:15 minutes |Serves 2

- 1 medium beet, peeled and sliced thin with a mandoline
- 2 tsp olive oil
- 1½ tsp Dill Seasoning Blend
- Salt to taste (optional)

1. Toss the beet slices in the olive oil (or aquafaba) and Dill Seasoning Blend. If you didn't add any salt to your dill seasoning, you add some now if you'd like or leave them salt-free.
2. Place a single layer in your air fryer basket. Cook at 330°F for 5 minutes. Separate pieces that are sticking together and give the basket a shake. I use tongs and crinkle up the individual slices.
3. Cook for 5 minutes more, repeat the separation of the beet slices and cook for a final 5 minutes.
4. If your beet slices are small in diameter, they may be done after the second 5 minutes; if large, they may need additional cooking time.

PER SERVING

Calories:114.8 | Fat:.9.1g |Carbs: 7.8g | Fiber: 2.3g | Protein: 1.3g

Crispy Beans

Prep time: 10 minutes | Cook time: 20 minutes | Serves 4

- 2 cans (15 oz.) of unsalted garbanzo beans
- ½ tsp. black pepper
- 1 tsp. garlic powder
- 1 tsp. onion powder
- 1 tsp. dried parsley flakes
- 2 tsp. dried dill
- cooking spray

1. At 400°F, preheat your air fryer.
2. Drain and rinse the beans in a strainer, then dry them with a kitchen towel.
3. Mix dill, parsley, onion powder, garlic powder, and black pepper in a small bowl.
4. Lightly grease a baking dish with cooking spray.
5. Spread the beans in the baking dish and grease the beans with cooking spray.
6. Drizzle the spice mixture over the beans and shake them to coat evenly.
7. Air fry the garbanzo beans for 20 minutes and shake after every 5 minutes.
8. Allow the beans to cool, then serve.

PER SERVING

Calories: 64 | Fat: 1g | Carbs: 11.6g | Protein: 3.7g | Fiber: 1g

Garlic Cauliflower Florets

Prep time: 10 Minutes | Cook time: 20 minutes | Serves 4

- 5 cups cauliflower florets
- 6 garlic cloves, chopped
- 4 tbsp. olive oil
- 1/2 tsp. cumin powder
- 1/2 tsp. salt

1. Add all ingredients into the large bowl and toss well.
2. Add them to the Air Fryer basket. Set to "Air Fry" at 400°F and cook for 20 minutes.

PER SERVING

Calories: 158.9 | Fat: 14.12 g | Carbs:8.21 g|Protein: 4g | Fiber: 2g

Cheesy Hot Sauce Collard Chips

Prep time: 30 minutes | Cook time:60 minutes |Serves 6

5 or 6 large collard leaves, stems removed and torn into bite-size pieces

- 4 cups torn
- 1 tsp mild oil or a few sprays of spray oil
- 1 tbsp nutritional yeast
- 1 tsp hot sauce (use as mild or hot as you prefer)
- ¼ tsp salt (or less if your hot sauce is very salty)

1. Wash the collards well, then dry in a salad spinner or with a clean dish towel. Place in a large mixing bowl. Depending on what method you use, either spray with oil or drizzle the oil (or aquafaba) on the collards.
2. Massage the collards to spread the oil evenly, then sprinkle the nutritional yeast, hot sauce and salt on ½ tsp. at a time and mix, repeating until everything is mixed well. Add the collards to your air fryer basket.
3. Set the temperature to 390°F and cook 5 minutes, and when the time is up, shake or gently stir the collard chips. Cook an additional 2 to 3 minutes.
4. If your chips aren't as crisp as you'd like them to be at this point, shake again and cook for 30-second to 1-minute intervals until they are. Be very careful because they go from almost done to burned quickly. I would not recommend cooking for more than 1 minute at this point.
5. The time will vary depending on the size and model of your air fryer. Store in an airtight container.

PER SERVING

Calories:120.7 | Fat: 5.0g |Carbs: 15.3g | Fiber: 8.1g |Protein: 7.2g

Kale Chips with Tex-Mex Dip

Prep time: 10 minutes | Cook time: 5 to 6 minutes | Serves 8

- 1 cup Greek yogurt
- 1 tbsp. chili powder
- ⅓ cup low-sodium salsa, well drained
- 1 bunch curly kale
- 1 tsp. olive oil
- ¼ tsp. coarse sea salt

1. In a small bowl, combine the yogurt, chili powder, and drained salsa; refrigerate.
2. Rinse the kale thoroughly, and pat dry. Remove the stems and ribs from the kale, using a sharp knife. Cut or tear the leaves into 3-inch pieces.
3. Toss the kale with the olive oil in a large bowl.
4. Air-fry the kale in small batches until the leaves are crisp. This should take 5 to 6 minutes. Shake the basket once during cooking time.
5. As you remove the kale chips, sprinkle them with a bit of the sea salt.
6. When all of the kale chips are done, serve with the dip.

PER SERVING
Calories: 35|Fat: 1g| Protein: 4g| Carbs: 2g| Fiber: 1g

Appendix 1 Measurement Conversion Chart

Volume Equivalents (Dry)

US STANDARD	METRIC (APPROXIMATE)
1/8 teaspoon	0.5 mL
1/4 teaspoon	1 mL
1/2 teaspoon	2 mL
3/4 teaspoon	4 mL
1 teaspoon	5 mL
1 tablespoon	15 mL
1/4 cup	59 mL
1/2 cup	118 mL
3/4 cup	177 mL
1 cup	235 mL
2 cups	475 mL
3 cups	700 mL
4 cups	1 L

Volume Equivalents (Liquid)

US STANDARD	US STANDARD (OUNCES)	METRIC (AP-PROXIMATE)
2 tablespoons	1 fl.oz.	30 mL
1/4 cup	2 fl.oz.	60 mL
1/2 cup	4 fl.oz.	120 mL
1 cup	8 fl.oz.	240 mL
1 1/2 cup	12 fl.oz.	355 mL
2 cups or 1 pint	16 fl.oz.	475 mL
4 cups or 1 quart	32 fl.oz.	1 L
1 gallon	128 fl.oz.	4 L

Temperatures Equivalents

FAHRENHEIT(F)	CELSIUS(C) APPROXIMATE)
225 °F	107 °C
250 °F	120 ° °C
275 °F	135 °C
300 °F	150 °C
325 °F	160 °C
350 °F	180 °C
375 °F	190 °C
400 °F	205 °C
425 °F	220 °C
450 °F	235 °C
475 °F	245 °C
500 °F	260 °C

Weight Equivalents

US STANDARD	METRIC (APPROXIMATE)
1 ounce	28 g
2 ounces	57 g
5 ounces	142 g
10 ounces	284 g
15 ounces	425 g
16 ounces (1 pound)	455 g
1.5 pounds	680 g
2 pounds	907 g

Appendix 2 The Dirty Dozen and Clean Fifteen

The Environmental Working Group (EWG) is a nonprofit, nonpartisan organization dedicated to protecting human health and the environment Its mission is to empower people to live healthier lives in a healthier environment. This organization publishes an annual list of the twelve kinds of produce, in sequence, that have the highest amount of pesticide residue-the Dirty Dozen-as well as a list of the fifteen kinds ofproduce that have the least amount of pesticide residue-the Clean Fifteen.

THE DIRTY DOZEN	
The 2016 Dirty Dozen includes the following produce. These are considered among the year's most important produce to buy organic:	
Strawberries	Spinach
Apples	Tomatoes
Nectarines	Bell peppers
Peaches	Cherry tomatoes
Celery	Cucumbers
Grapes	Kale/collard greens
Cherries	Hot peppers

The Dirty Dozen list contains two additional itemskale/collard greens and hot peppers-because they tend to contain trace levels of highly hazardous pesticides.

THE CLEAN FIFTEEN	
The least critical to buy organically are the Clean Fifteen list. The following are on the 2016 list:	
Avocados	Papayas
Corn	Kiw
Pineapples	Eggplant
Cabbage	Honeydew
Sweet peas	Grapefruit
Onions	Cantaloupe
Asparagus	Cauliflower
Mangos	

Some of the sweet corn sold in the United States are made from genetically engineered (GE) seedstock. Buy organic varieties of these crops to avoid GE produce.

Appendix 3 Index

Hey there!

Wow, can you believe we've reached the end of this culinary journey together? I'm truly thrilled and filled with joy as I think back on all the recipes we've shared and the flavors we've discovered. This experience, blending a bit of tradition with our own unique twists, has been a journey of love for good food. and knowing you've been out there, giving these dishes a try, has made this adventure incredibly special to me.

Even though we're turning the last page of this book, I hope our conversation about all things delicious doesn't have to end. I cherish your thoughts, your experiments, and yes, even those moments when things didn't go as planned. Every piece of feedback you share is invaluable, helping to enrich this experience for us all.

I'd be so grateful if you could take a moment to share your thoughts with me, be it through a review on Amazon or any other place you feel comfortable expressing yourself online. Whether it's praise, constructive criticism, or even an idea for how we might do things differently in the future, your input is what truly makes this journey meaningful.

This book is a piece of my heart, offered to you with all the love and enthusiasm I have for cooking. But it's your engagement and your words that elevate it to something truly extraordinary.

Thank you from the bottom of my heart for being such an integral part of this culinary adventure. Your openness to trying new things and sharing your experiences has been the greatest gift.

Catch you later,

Elizabeth E. Wright

Made in the USA
Monee, IL
20 December 2024

74896689R00044